Isaiah Price

Reunion of the Ninety-Seventh Regiment Pennsylvania Volunteers, October 29th, 1884

At Camp Wayne, West Chester, Pa. An account of the proceedings with a

roster of the comrades present

Isaiah Price

Reunion of the Ninety-Seventh Regiment Pennsylvania Volunteers, October 29th, 1884
At Camp Wayne, West Chester, Pa. An account of the proceedings with a roster of the comrades present

ISBN/EAN: 9783337426132

Printed in Europe, USA, Canada, Australia, Japan

Cover: Foto ©ninafisch / pixelio.de

More available books at **www.hansebooks.com**

REUNION

OF THE

NINETY-SEVENTH REGIMENT

PENNSYLVANIA VOLUNTEERS,

OCTOBER 29th, 1884,

"ON THE OLD CAMP GROUND,"

AT CAMP WAYNE, WEST CHESTER, PA.

--- --- ---

AN ACCOUNT OF THE PROCEEDINGS

WITH

A ROSTER OF THE COMRADES PRESENT

PREPARED BY

BREVET-COLONEL ISAIAH PRICE,

Companion of the Military Order of the Loyal Legion of the
United States. Comrade of George G. Meade,
Post No. 1, Dept. Penna. G. A. R.

AUTHOR OF THE

HISTORY OF THE NINETY-SEVENTH REGIMENT P. V.

PHILADELPHIA, 1884.

PRESS OF
DONALDSON & MAGRATH,
614 SANSOM ST.

REUNION

OF THE

NINETY-SEVENTH REGIMENT PENNSYLVANIA VOLUNTEERS.

PREPARATORY PROCEEDINGS.

WEST CHESTER, PA., February 2d, 1884.

The surviving members of the Ninety-seventh Regiment Pennsylvania Volunteers are requested to meet at the Green Tree Hotel, West Chester, on Saturday, February 23d, 1884, for the purpose of providing for a Reunion between the members yet living. All interested are invited to attend. [Signed] LOUIS Y. EVANS,
R. BRUCE WALLACE.

WEST CHESTER, PA., February 23d, 1884.

Pursuant to the foregoing call, published in the *Local News* of this place, and signed by Lewis Y. Evans of Coatesville and by R. Bruce Wallace of Philadelphia, seventeen survivors of the Ninety-seventh Regiment, Pennsylvania Volunteers, assembled at 2 o'clock this P. M. at the Green Tree Hotel in this borough.

By the terms of the call the meeting was for the purpose of taking measures to bring about a Reunion of the Regiment as soon as practicable.

The following were present :

Captain F. M. Guss, Co. A,
Captain Leonard R. Thomas, Co. C,
Sergeant Isaac A. Cleaver, Co. C,
Private John J. Still, Co. C,
Private Oliver B. Channell, Co. C,
Private Samuel A. March, Co. C,
Quartermaster David Jones,
Fife-Major C. C. Fahnestock,
Sergeant George L. Smith, Co. E,
Brevet-Lieutenant-Colonel D. W. C. Lewis, Co. F,
Private Evan Pharaoh, Co. F,
Corporal Barnett R. Rapp, Co. K.

On motion the following officers were appointed : Isaac A. Cleaver, chairman ; Oliver B. Channell, treasurer, and Leonard R. Thomas, secretary.

It was moved and seconded that a Reunion be held as soon as it can be brought about. Agreed to.

On motion it was resolved to call a preliminary meeting of the survivors, to be held in Cabinet Hall, West Chester, at 2 P. M., May 3d, 1884.

To assist the secretary in procuring the names and addresses of surviving comrades, the following named were appointed : Samuel A. March, David Jones, Geo. L. Smith and Evan Pharaoh.

A subscription amounting to $5.50 was raised to defray the expenses of correspondence.

On motion adjourned.

L. R. THOMAS, Secretary.

PROCEEDINGS OF MEETING MAY 3d, 1884.

THE NINETY-SEVENTH PENNSYLVANIA VOLUNTEERS.

After many years they meet again in West Chester.

The preliminary meeting for the furtherance of the proposed Reunion of the old Ninety-seventh Regiment, Pennsylvania Volunteers, held in West Chester, Saturday afternoon, May 3d, 1884, was attended by sixty-nine survivors of that well-known military body, which went forth from here in the cause of the Union more than a score of years ago. The meeting was an enthusiastic one in every respect, its deliberations being characterized by the best of good feeling, giving evidence that hereafter the bonds of brotherhood are to be more strongly united among the remaining comrades. At 2.30 o'clock I. A. Cleaver rapped the assemblage to order, and stated what had been done in order to gather the boys together once more. The temporary secretary read the minutes of the previous meeting, held in the Green Tree Hotel, a full account of which has been published. Suffice it to say that at that gathering there were seventeen of the comrades, who elected as temporary officers I. A. Cleaver, president; L. R. Thomas, secretary, and O. B. Channell, treasurer; "that the secretary was authorized to communicate with all the old members of the regiment whose post-office addresses he could secure, in reference to the proposed Reunion, and also to call a meeting of the same for that purpose, to be held on May 3d in the Cabinet Hall, West Chester." The minutes were approved as read.

Colonel Isaiah Price then arose, and in a few well-chosen remarks stated that he hoped the good work commenced, would result in such an organization of the old members of the Ninety-seventh as would reflect credit upon it and place on a firm basis an association that would survive until the last man of them had gone to meet the spirits of those who had fallen in battle by their comrades' sides some twenty years ago. He was glad to see so many of them about him looking hale and hearty ; was happy to notice that great interest had been taken in the movement ; he wanted a society formed in which they could all meet annually to talk over by-gone times and relate camp-fire reminiscences, besides the gathering together and keeping intact all records and historical papers relating to the Regiment during its service in the war. He concluded by moving that a committee of five be appointed to prepare a constitution and by-laws to govern the proposed association. His remarks were loudly applauded and his motion heartily approved by the comrades. The chair then named Colonel Price, L. R. Thomas, R. B. Wallace, E. L. Schofield and D. W. C. Lewis to serve as a committee for that purpose. They were also instructed to name suitable persons for permanent officers of the association, during their deliberations, whose names could afterward be submitted to the meeting for action. The committee then retired, and the chair appointed Serg't-Major Hawley to officiate as secretary in the absence of L. R. Thomas, who was appointed on the committee.

A list of the names of the members present was then desired, when a member proposed that the old roll be called. The chair stated that, as the roll was not at hand, and that it would only revive sad memories to hear comrades' names mentioned who were dead and gone, it were best that two or three of those present go among the members and get their names and addresses, also company letter, which was done with the following result :

FIELD OFFICERS.

Colonel H. R. Guss, Brevet-Colonel Isaiah Price, Surgeon John R. Everhart, Quartermaster David Jones, all of West Chester.

NON-COMMISSIONED STAFF.

Sergeant-Major Samuel W. Hawley, Media ; Fife-Major Casper C. Fahnestock, West Chester.

CO. A.

Captain F. M. Guss, First Lieutenant Abel Griffith, West Chester ; First Lieutenant Harry T. Gray and Private Edward R. Eisenbeis, Philadelphia ; Alexander M. Chandler, Spread Eagle, Chester Co. ; John A. Groff, West Chester.

CO. B.

Corporal R. Bruce Wallace, Philadelphia ; Private Samuel Miles, West Chester.

6

CO. C.

Captain Leonard R. Thomas, First Lieutenants Emmor G. Griffith, West Chester, and George W. Able, Concordville, Delaware Co.; Sergeants Isaac A. Cleaver, Berwyn; Stephen H. Eachus, West Chester, B. Lundy Kent (Captain Eighteenth Heavy Artillery, U. S. C. T.), Wilmington, Del.; Corporals Jesse D. Farra, Davis O. Taylor, and Privates Samuel A. March, Oliver B. Channell and Emmor B. Hickman, West Chester; J. Jones Still, Malvern; William D. Thomas, Downingtown; James J. Dewees, New Centreville; George W. Walton, Philadelphia; Isaac Paschall, Newtown Square, Delaware Co.

CO. D.

Corporal Robert Fairlamb, Elwyn, Delaware Co.; Privates Walter Pyle, Cheyney, Delaware Co.; Abraham Fawkes, East Whiteland; Wm. McIntosh, Downingtown.

CO. E.

Sergeant Geo. L. Smith, Musician Charles Riley, Jr., West Chester; Privates Michael Connor, Malvern; James A. Riley, Coatesville; George W. Eavenson, Thornton, Delaware Co.

CO. F.

Captain and Brevet-Lieutenant-Colonel D. W. C. Lewis, First Lieutenant Thomas Cosgriff, West Chester; Sergeant Samuel Wynn, Nantmeal Village; Herman P. Brower, West Whiteland; Corporal Jesse M. Boyles and Private Evan Pharaoh, West Chester; Privates Eli Reynolds, Birdsboro', Berks Co.; William E. Stiteler, Columbia, Pa.

CO. G.

Captain Caleb Hoopes, Media; Second Lieutenants Joseph M. Borrell and William H. Eves, Chester, Delaware Co.; Sergeants Charles E. Ottey, Media, Charles Gray, and Corporals John S. Culbert, Joseph R. Parsons, Chester, Delaware Co., and Hillery Fox, West Chester, Pa., and Private Crosley B. Wilson, Media.

CO. H.

Captain George A. Lemaistre, Wilmington, Del.; Musicians Charles C. Taylor, William Dallings, and Teamster Marshall B. England, West Chester; Privates Alfred C. Allison, Downingtown; Abia C. E. Miller, Philadelphia, and William M. Steele, Phœnixville.

CO. I.

Private James Groff, Clifton Heights, Delaware Co.

CO. K.

Captain William Wayne, Paoli, and First Lieutenant William M. Sullivan, Warren Tavern; Corporals William Taylor, Woodstown, N. J.; Barnett R. Rapp, West Chester; E. Lane Schofield, Paoli, and Private William Miles, Willistown. Total, 69 comrades.

During this feature of the proceedings the men could not retain their composure, it had been so long since they had an opportunity of greeting one another in that way. Hands were shaken again and again, shoulders were slapped, jokes were cracked, compliments were exchanged, and a running fire of merriment was kept up, much to the annoyance of the comrades who were trying to secure the list of their names.

One old man, who had come in his regimental uniform, stood in the doorway and fairly laughed with joy at the sight of so many faces he knew so well. He was older than any of the rest of them, but his spirits were just as light as in the days when he " drank from the same canteen" with those around him. His long white hair peeped out nicely from beneath the " sojer cap " on his head, which familiar tile he at last, in the exhuberance of his spirits, pulled off and gave three rousing cheers for " the old Ninety-seventh."

The committee returned as the echoes of the old comrade's cheers died away, and reported the following constitution and by-laws :

CONSTITUTION.

I. The name of this association shall be " The Society of the Ninety-seventh Regiment of Pennsylvania Volunteers."

II. Any honorably discharged officer or soldier, who at any time has served in the said Ninety-seventh Regiment of Pennsylvania Volunteers, shall be entitled to membership in the Society.

III. The object of the Society shall be the promotion of kindly feeling, the revival of old associations, and the collection and preservation of records of the services rendered by this Regiment during the " War of the Rebellion."

IV. The officers of the Society shall consist of a president, three vice-presidents, secretary, treasurer and historian, who shall be, with the exception of the historian, elected at each annual meeting of the Society.

V. The duties of the president shall be to preside at the annual meetings, to call such other meetings of the Society as may be necessary, and to issue such orders as may be required for the good government and control of the Society.

VI. The first vice-president shall exercise the powers of the president in case of the absence of that officer.

VII. The secretary shall keep a record of the minutes of the proceedings of the Society, a roll of the members, and perform all duties usually pertaining to the office of secretary.

VIII. The treasurer shall have the custody of all funds, to be expended only on approval of the president, by an order drawn and countersigned by the secretary ; and he shall render an account of all disbursements at the annual meeting of the Society.

IX. The historian shall collect and preserve for the use of the Society such history of the Regiment and its service as may be obtainable, and such papers, records, etc., as may from time to time be added to the collection which may serve to preserve the record of the Regiment after its survivors shall have passed on to join those comrades who fell during the conflict.

X. An executive committee of five members shall be elected annually, who shall attend to the business of the Association during the intervals of its session.

XI. Having a fraternal feeling for and honoring the glorious efforts of our brothers in arms belonging to other regiments who have shared with us in service, the president, vice-presidents or any member shall be authorized to invite the attendance at our annual meeting of any officer or soldier of any sister regiment.

BY-LAWS.

I. The entrance fee of the Society shall be $1.00.

II. The annual dues shall be 50 cents, payable at the annual meeting.

III. The president shall determine the time and place of each annual meeting, being governed in his selections thereof as far as practicable by the time and place of meeting of the Society of the Army of the James or of the Tenth Army Corps, or other organizations with which our Regiment was identified.

IV. When the place for the next annual meeting shall have been decided upon, the president shall appoint three members, resident at or near the place, whose duty it shall be to assist the executive committee in making all needful arrangements and preparations for such meeting.

V. This Constitution and By-Laws may be altered and amended by a vote of two-thirds of the members present at any annual meeting, providing such alteration or amendment shall have been presented in writing at the previous annual meeting.

At the conclusion of the reading of the above constitution and by-laws, it was moved and seconded that they be adopted as read, which motion was carried unanimously. The committee then reported the names of the following comrades to fill the offices created by the constitution :

President, Colonel Henry R. Guss ; first vice-president, I. A.

Cleaver, C; second vice-president, Captain Wm. Wayne, K; third vice-president, Captain Caleb Hoopes, G; secretary, Captain L. R. Thomas, C; treasurer, William Taylor, K; executive committee, Sergeant-Major Samuel W. Hawley; Robert Fairlamb, D; Herman P. Brower, F; Lieutenant Wm. H. Eves, G; Captain Wm. S. Underwood, K.

The members named for the various offices were elected by acclamation.

Colonel Guss then took the chair, and after thanking his fellow comrades in arms for the honor conferred upon him in having been called upon to preside over their deliberations, he said he was ready to proceed to business. A short recess was here taken to allow members an opportunity to pay the entrance fee of $1, when the meeting was again called to order.

Comrade William Taylor, who had been elected treasurer, asked to be excused from serving on account of his living so far away from Chester County—at Woodstown, New Jersey. His request was accordingly granted, and Oliver B. Channell, West Chester, was elected treasurer of the Society.

The chair then named West Chester as the place and October 29th as the date for holding the Reunion, and appointed John A. Groff, S. A. March and B. R. Rapp as a committee to assist the executive committee in preparing for the event. The office of "historian" not having yet been filled, Colonel Isaiah Price's name was proposed, and he was elected by the voice of the entire assemblage.

A comrade then arose and proposed for honorary membership the name of Mrs. Mary St. John of Philadelphia, which was received with great applause. Her name was at once entered upon the books. Mrs. St. John, who was the wife of the Drum-Major, James St. John, joined the Regiment as they marched through Philadelphia, as laundress, her home being in the above city. Her two youngest sons were also members of the Regiment as drummer boys. She stayed with the Regiment until 1864, and rendered valuable service to the sick and wounded.

With the secretary asking the members present to send all names of the absent comrades they knew to him, the meeting adjourned amid much enthusiasm.

Comrades wishing to enroll as members of the Society will please send their names, with entrance fee, to the secretary, L. R. Thomas, West Chester, Pa.

The committee intend to hold reveille on the morning of the Reunion, in front of the Court House, from which point the Regiment will march to the place where the event is to be held; the exact spot, for holding the contemplated Reunion, being as yet not determined upon. The day chosen is the anniversary of the formal organization of the Regiment at Camp Wayne, West Chester, on October 29th, 1861.

MINUTES OF EXECUTIVE COMMITTEE.

WEST CHESTER, September 4th, 1884.

Pursuant to call of the chairman, the executive committee of the Society of the Ninety-seventh Regiment, Pennsylvania Volunteers, met at the office of John A. Groff at 2 P. M. Chairman S. W. Hawley presided. Present: Robert Fairlamb, W. S. Underwood, I. A. Cleaver, Wm. H. Eves, S. A. March and Colonel H. R. Guss.

A committee on music and one on decorations were appointed.

S. W. Hawley and L. R. Thomas were appointed to arrange for an orator and chaplain.

It was decided to provide a dinner, to be paid for from funds raised by subscription among the members of the Regiment.

S. A. March was appointed treasurer of the executive committee.

Adjourned to meet at same place at 2 P. M., September 19th.

L. R. THOMAS, *Secretary.*

WEST CHESTER, September 19th, 1884.

The executive committee met at the time and place appointed, S. W. Hawley presiding. Most of the committee, with B. R. Rapp, S. A. March and John A. Groff of the assistant committee, present. Colonel Guss and others gave their advice and assistance. It was resolved to hold the exercises of the Reunion at the Fair Grounds. John A. Groff was appointed to ascertain the terms upon which the use thereof could be had.

The committee on orator and chaplain reported that Chaplain D. W. Moore would attend and officiate ; and that Comrade Marriott Brosius had accepted the invitation to deliver the oration. The other committees reported progress. John A. Groff was appointed to get estimates of the cost of furnishing dinner for one hundred and fifty, to be gotten up in a style suitable to the occasion.

It was decided to have appropriate toasts prepared, to be read and responded to at the banquet on the occasion of the Reunion.

Committee then adjourned to meet at the office of John A. Groff at 2 P. M., October 3d, 1884. L. R. THOMAS, *Secretary.*

WEST CHESTER, October 3d, 1884.

The executive committee met at the time and place appointed. Chairman Hawley presided. Present: John A. Groff, H. P. Brower, W. H. Eves, W. S. Underwood, L. R. Thomas, S. A. March and David Jones.

It was resolved to have the dinner served in the Agricultural Building at the Fair Grounds. Committee on decorations reported progress. On music progress. On Fair Grounds reported they can be had for $10.00. Report was accepted and committee discharged. Mr. Groff reported an estimate for the dinner in accordance with a bill of fare adopted by the committee, to be placed upon the table with proper attendants, as follows: For 150 plates, $1.75 per plate; for 200 plates, $1.50 per plate. On motion the last estimate was accepted, and the order given to furnish and serve properly in accordance with the bill of fare for two hundred plates for the dinner on October 29th at the Fair Grounds. S. A. March was appointed a committee to arrange the tables, etc., in the building selected. The programme was substantially arranged as follows:

Comrades to meet at the grounds at 11 A. M. Oct. 29th, 1884. Business meeting from 11 A. M. to 12 M.; oration from 12 to 1 P. M. or after; dinner from 1.30 to 2.30 P. M. The secretary was authorized to have 300 copies of the programme printed, including the bill of fare, and directed to send one to every survivor whom he could reach. D. W. C. Lewis agreed to see that the stand for the purpose of the exercises and the oration should be erected in time. Committee adjourned to meet at 2 P. M. on Oct. 25th, at Mr. Groff's office.

L. R. THOMAS, *Secretary.*

WEST CHESTER, October 25th, 1884.

An adjourned meeting of the executive committee was held at the time and place appointed. Chairman Hawley presided. Present: Comrades Underwood, Fairlamb, Eves, March, Rapp, Colonel H. R. Guss, I. A. Cleaver, H. C. Reagan and others.

Committee on music reported that Dr. H. C. Wood's Orchestra had been engaged to perform for the occasion at a price not to exceed $25.00; the members of the orchestra to have dinner free.

Committee on decorations reported having made arrangements to have the work done at a cost of $25.00 or thereabouts.

Colonel D. W. C. Lewis and Major D. Jones were appointed a committee to extend a proper reception to the orator of the day, Comrade Brosius, and to receive Mrs. St. John with carriage at depot and convey her to the grounds. Adjourned to meet at call of chairman. L. R. THOMAS, *Secretary.*

Reunion of the Ninety-Seventh Regiment, Penna. Volunteers,

AT WEST CHESTER, PA., OCTOBER 29TH, 1884.

The day set apart, and long anticipated, for this interesting event opened with skies overcast with gray clouds, that yet lingered from the stormy day preceding, as though typical of the clouds and storms of war from which the remnant about to meet had emerged twenty-three years ago, "when the curtain fell upon the Drama of the Rebellion," permitting the survivors of the war to return to their homes and receive the grateful welcome that there awaited them.

By 9 o'clock the streets of the town were occupied by groups of bronzed-faced, sturdy men, who had arrived by train or other conveyances, and taking their way toward the central point of gravitation, the old "Headquarters" at the "Green Tree," halted by the way at corners of streets when meeting other familiar faces of like acquaintance with the "signs of service," and having the same earnest gaze in quest of recognition of some old comrade, in the whitened locks of more than twenty years' bleaching; then the mutual recall between long-separated comrades, of the traces of the younger face in each, that caused the rush together, and the grasp of hand, and the "How are you, old boy?" and the "Well, I declare, if that ain't my old bunk-mate! I shouldn't have known you for the young rooster that used to play off your pranks on the boys." So here goes for the old game of ear-pulling and the thumps, and the "ayau!" with which the old camp used to resound.

Such were some of the first retouchings of elbows that initiated the reassembling in front of the Colonel's old hostelry as in the former days. And here the comrades continued to assemble as the morning hours wore on, the greetings becoming more and more numerous and cordial. One would point out to another—"There is Dave M. Taylor of Co. A, cashier of the Oxford Bank;" or "Captain Dallas Crow, Co. B. He handles the money of the Adams Express Company in Philadelphia now. And here is Corporal Davis O. Taylor of Co. C, who is running before the people, as he never ran before the enemy, for the office of Clerk of the Courts of Chester County, and sure to win at that. And over there by that corner post is Walter Pyle of Co. D, who can still build a

stone wall to stay, as he did in his younger days—solid to the front
in every duty as a soldier and a master mason. Co. E is repre-
sented over yonder by Sergeant Signet of Phœnixville, who works
now amid the grime and smoke of the iron furnaces there, as in the
old days he did in the trenches before Wagner under the smoke of
rebel guns. Who could expect to recognize Sergeant Herman P.
Brower of Co. F, who had counted but eighteen years when he
shouldered his musket, and didn't tire of it in '64, but re-enlisted for
the war, and now, after twenty-three years' wear has added to his eighteen, the man of forty-one might easily be passed without any of
the boys picking him out, but the touch of palm and the glance of
the eye entitle him to " the pass-word and the grip."
A pair of bright black eyes look out from a solid smooth face, upon
which a smile is seen as he grasps the hand of one standing near him,
and he says," You don't know me; do you, captain?" There is a famili-
arity in the features that tells of a boy full of fun and mischief, with a
smartness that could often circumvent the closest watchfulness of superior officers, more to their annoyance than any very serious consequence! Yes, that eye and that glance, with the cordial smile of
greeting must belong to young Sullivan of Co. H! The pleasure of
his remembrance and proffered greeting was one of the brightest incidents of the day. The man matured from the soldier boy is one
worthy of full comradeship with his fellow survivors of the war. He
became a good soldier and now helps to build ships as a machinist
at Wilmington, Del. And there is Pioneer Snyder of Co. G, whose
tall form shows his unchanged face beaming with the delight of meeting so many who have not forgotten his familiar features.
Over there Lindsay of Co. I is hunting up some of " the squad,"
and he will find them on hand sure, as they always put in an appear-
ance when wanted, brave and sturdy and with much of the vigor of
their brave and lamented captain, Hawkins.
The boys of the " Honorable Member's " Company, and he too,
are on hand, and Captain Underwood has succeeded in reorgan-
izing the old drum corps for the occasion, and Cass Fahnestock
and Riley are about to sound the "call for the assembling."
At a quarter to 11 o'clock Major Price called upon the boys
" to fall in." Promptly the veterans took their places in the ranks,
while the crowd of lookers-on remained upon the sidewalks interested spectators of " forming the line." As the men separated from
the crowd, and stood again in solid phalanx together, the *esprit de
corps* was renewed as if by magic, and the old martial bearing

returned, bridging the interval of the years of peaceful pursuits and bringing back in vivid realization the influence of the soldier's ready obedience to the command of "Attention!" "Forward March!" taking up the step at the sound of the same fife and drum that had so often called them forth to the march and the field of battle. Captain W. S. Underwood conducted the music on the right. Colonel John Wainwright and Brevet-Colonel Isaiah Price led the one hundred and sixty-eight officers and men, who then marched out Gay Street to Church, down Church Street to the Fair Grounds, where they were met by Colonel Guss and Lieutenant-Colonel A. P. Duer, the committee of arrangements and the special committee having charge of the reception of the orator of the day, Hon. Marriott Brosius; and Mrs. St. John and daughter, had preceded the veterans to the place of meeting in carriages, and also about forty of the comrades who had previously walked to the grounds. The battalion was halted in front of the stand, erected in rear of the track stand, for the exercises of the day. It was appropriately draped with the national flag, having an awning canopy, and a beautiful bouquet of flowers upon the table.

Announcement was then made requesting the men of the different companies to assemble in groups and proceed to register their names and post-office addresses with the secretary of the association, Captain Leonard R. Thomas, who occupied the managers' office adjacent to the stand for this purpose.

During this proceeding the president of the association, Colonel H. R. Guss, accompanied by the orator of the day, Hon. Marriott Brosius, Second Lieutenant of Co. K; Colonel John Wainwright, Rev. David W. Moore, Chaplain; and Brevet-Colonel Isaiah Price, historian of the Regiment, occupied the platform. Soon after taking their seats the reception committee, Colonel D. W. C. Lewis and Major David Jones, brought to the stand Mother St. John, comfortably wrapped from the cold, and seated her in a large rocking-chair in the presence of the comrades, who greeted her with three hearty cheers.

Colonel Guss called the meeting to order, and said :

Comrades of the Ninety-seventh Regiment and Mother St. John :
It affords me much pleasure to welcome you here upon the First Reunion of our old Regiment, hoping to have the pleasure of seeing you and many more members of the old Regiment at our future meetings. Knowing many of your number have traveled many miles to be with us this day, shows the interest you have taken in

the meeting. Hoping this interest may grow with all, many thanks for your presence here to-day, and hoping you may all have a very pleasant day and one you will long remember with pleasure, I now introduce the Chaplain of the Regiment, Rev. D. W. Moore, who will open the exercises with prayer.

The Chaplain then came forward and offered the following beautiful and touching address to the throne of Grace:

PRAYER BY THE CHAPLAIN.

O thou who art the Lord God of the heavens above and the earth beneath; thou Creator of all things therein, and thou who art *our* kind Preserver and most merciful Benefactor, we would not assemble *here* and *now* without seeking thy benediction.

O Lord, thou hast been very good to us, in that thou hast spared us to come together to-day, after many years of separation and of varied vicissitudes, since we were together as soldiers fighting the battles of our beloved country, and for which many of our original numbers fell dead on the field of carnage; or died in hospitals, nursed by loving hearts and tender hands, at home; or in the horrible prisons of the South, with nothing to comfort or cheer their dying hours. O Lord, we have not forgotten the many trying experiences of the past, nor would we ever forget them. Especially would we remember that " thy banner over us has been love." And we render thee thanks this day for all of thy goodness and gracious dealings. And we thank thee, O Lord, for the preservation of our country—for the Union of these States—and for the overthrow of Rebellion.

And we do most earnestly beseech thee to continue thy favor unto this our native land. Suffer no enemy to invade our shores, and keep us from destroying ourselves by internal strifes and political seditions. O thou God of our Revolutionary fathers, grant us thy grace, and their spirit of patriotism, which will lead us as a people to make sacrifices of all personal and party considerations for the good and perpetuity of the nation at large.

And now, O Lord, will thou forgive us of our many sins, both as soldiers and as people? We all have sinned and come short of the glory of the Lord. In thy rich grace and mercy pardon us of all transgressions, and lift up the light of thy countenance and smile upon all of us who are here to-day. And forget not to bless the soldier's widow and his orphan children. Be good and kind,

O Lord, to those who have suffered the loss of all that was dear to them for the sake of our American liberties.

Hear, O Lord, and answer these our feeble supplications, and save us all in thy kingdom above, for Jesus' sake. Amen.

Colonel Guss then stated the first business in order would be the reading of the proceedings of the meetings preliminary to this one, at which the Association of the Ninety-seventh Regiment was formed, and which had fixed upon the time and place of holding this Reunion; but as the secretary of the association was now engaged in making the registry of the names of the comrades, he would call upon the historian of the Regiment, Brevet-Colonel Isaiah Price, to read a paper he had prepared for this occasion.

The following is the historical sketch read at the Reunion by Colonel Price :

REUNION NINETY-SEVENTH REGIMENT P. V.

October 29th, 1884.

Comrades ! As your historian, entrusted with the duty of pre-serving the record of service in which our Regiment participated during the war of the Rebellion, it is with a degree of satisfaction commensurate with the pride we all may indulge in feeling, from having borne a part in those services, in whatever station, that I may refer you to the published record it was my privilege to prepare ten years ago, of which I need only say, some of your number have given me the best assurances of *their* appreciation of its interest to them.

That narrative brings the account down to the close of the war, the return of the discharged veterans to receive the well-deserved, honored welcome from their fellow-citizens, friends, and their anx-iously-expectant families, parents, sisters, brothers and lovers.

It contains also the record roll of each man's service in detail, whether found among those of you who returned to claim and receive the glad welcome that awaited you, or with the long list of those who laid down life for their country! whom we left upon the field of battle to sleep the calm, eternal sleep in which repose those devoted patriot martyrs.

It also gives the proceedings had in regard to the erection of the proposed monument, so long the subject of conjecture and criti-cism regarding its completion. The delay is therein explained as due to the objections, as to location, on the part of the residents in or owners of the properties adjacent to the site that was formally designated by the borough authorities for its erection—on the west line of Church Street, in the middle of Market Street, on a plot twelve feet square, enclosed by an iron railing.

Trusting that in time this opposition would be withdrawn, the trustees of the monument fund, who are charged with the duty of building the monument, have quietly waited for some evidence of such change of feeling in regard to that location.

Nearly two years ago the subject was again revived by the trustees and the secretary of the Monument Association, when in view of the continued opposition to the proposed site, another was suggested as available, although all are united in opinion that no other in West Chester could be so appropriate or desirable as the one already designated.

Having ascertained that the lot on which the old basin is located is no longer required by the borough for that purpose and was to be leveled and added to "Marshall Square," the trustees with the secretary joined in petitioning the borough council of last year to grant them the western half of that lot with the foundation of half the old basin as a site for the monument, at such time as the council should be prepared to abandon its present use. The proposition was favorably entertained by a portion of the members, but the majority at that time was not inclined to favor monument building. Action was therefore deferred to await a more auspicious consideration. The incoming of the board of the present year gave expectation of greater favor for our application. This has been verified by the assurances received that the present board are united in purpose to grant our request when the material of the present basin shall be removed, as it is required for use in other borough improvements.

The trustees will accordingly proceed with the erection of the monument at that locality, when the ground shall be made ready for its reception. The delay, it will be seen, has been of such unavoidable nature as to attach no censure to the trustees, who have been ready and willing to comply with the duties of their trust, at all times since their appointment.

It will be unnecessary to recount in this paper the proceedings preliminary to the present reunion of the members of the regiment, as these are already recorded in the minutes of the meetings previously held by the secretary thereof, and in the recorded action of the committee appointed to prepare for these interesting ceremonies in which we are now engaged.

The only remaining duty for the historian will consist in collecting and recording such individual accounts of those who have fulfilled the record of life, as may become known to him, that each record may be filled out to the final discharge, so that future generations may know who were the last to respond to the "roll call" when all shall be assembled in that final meeting of "the grand army above."

The account thus collected will also embrace the mention of such public service or position as may be occupied by any of our number, or whatever matter of public interest may come to the notice of the historian. It will greatly assist these labors if each member of the regiment will forward to his address at West Chester, Pa., a brief record of the time and place of death, nature of disease, etc., of any of our number that may be known at any time by him, and also any fact of public interest such as is indicated herein.

The first name calling for our notice is one distinguished in the service of his country, whom we all honor for his brave deeds and pity for his painful wounds received while with us in the volunteer defence of our country, while yet a lad, displaying those qualities of the true soldier which have entitled him to receive the distinguished recognition of an appointment rarely accorded outside the training received at West Point. Following his record in the U. S. Army from the point at which it is left in the history of the regiment, General Pennypacker has commanded as follows:

1874. Commanding Sixteenth Infantry and Post of Nashville, January to August. Commanding U. S. troops in New Orleans ("Overturning of the Kellogg State Government"), September and October. Commanding Sixteenth Infantry and Post of Nashville, November and December. President General Court Martial at Lebanon, Ky., in April. Same duty at Nashville in May.

1875. Commanding Sixteenth Infantry and Post of Nashville, January to December, including President General Court-martial at Mobile in August. Commanding escort, funeral of President Johnson, at Nashville, October 2d.

1876. Commanding Sixteenth Infantry and Post of Nashville, January to June. Commanding military escort at funeral of Major-General Gordon Granger, at Lexington, Ky., January 25th, 1876. Commanding Department of the South, with headquarters at Louisville, Ky., July, August and September. Commanding Sixteenth Infantry and Newport Barracks, Ky., October. Commanding Sixteenth Infantry and Mount Vernon Barracks, Ala., November. Commanding Sixteenth Infantry and U. S. troops in Custom-house, New Orleans (during the "electoral count"), December.

1877. Commanding Sixteenth Infantry and U. S. troops in Custom-house, New Orleans, January to June. Commanding Sixteenth Infantry and Fort Riley, Kan., July to December. President General Court-martial, Fort Lyon, Col., August and September. Member General Court-martial, Fort Union, New Mexico, December.

1878. Commanding Sixteenth Infantry and Fort Riley, Kan., January to December inclusive. Member of Retiring Board at Fort Leavenworth, Kan., October, November and December.

1879. Commanding Sixteenth Infantry and Fort Riley, Kan., January to March. President Court of Inquiry at Fort Stanton, New Mexico ("the Lincoln County murder"), April, May, June, July and August. Member General Court-martial at Fort Leavenworth, Kan., September. Commanding Sixteenth Infantry and Fort Riley, Kan., October, November and December. Member General Court-martial, Fort Riley, Kan., October and November.

1880. Commanding Sixteenth Infantry and Fort Riley, Kan., January to October. President General Court-martial, San Antonio, Texas, November. Commanding Sixteenth Infantry and Post of San Antonio, December.

1881. Commanding Sixteenth Infantry and Post of San Antonio, Texas, January to April. Commanding Sixteenth Infantry and Fort McKavett, Texas, May to December. President General Court-martial, Fort Davis, Texas (for the trial of Lieutenant Flipper, "the colored officer of the army"), September, October, November and December.

1882. Commanding Sixteenth Infantry and Fort McKavett, Texas, January to June. On leave of absence and in Europe (on surgeon's certificate of disability on account of wounds received in battle), July to December.

1883. On leave of absence and in Europe, January to May. Transferred from the active to the retired list of the Regular Army, by direction of the President of the United States, July 3d, 1883, on account of disability arising from severe wounds received in action.

1884. Residence in Philadelphia.

Brevet-Colonel Isaiah Price. Having made application to the War Department for muster upon his commission as Major, received while in command of the Regiment at Cold Harbor, Va., in June, 1864, being then and subsequently prevented from muster by the absence, wounded, of Colonel Pennypacker, the following order was issued granting the application :

Special Order No. 277.　　HEADQUARTERS OF THE ARMY, ADJUTANT-GENERAL'S OFFICE,
WASHINGTON, D. C., December 4th, 1883.

EXTRACT.

*　　*　　*　　*　　*　　*　　*　　*

2. By direction of the Secretary of War, under the joint resolution approved July 11th, 1870 (amendatory of the joint resolution
approved July 26th, 1866), and to complete his record, the muster-
out of service of Captain Isaiah Price, Company C, Ninety-seventh
Pennsylvania Volunteers, September 17th, 1864, is amended to take
effect June 6th, 1864. He is mustered into service as Major of said
Regiment to date June 7th, 1864, and mustered out and honorably
discharged as Major to date September 17th, 1864, and he is
mustered for pay in said grade during the period embraced between
the aforesaid dates. The amount of pay and allowances received
by him as Captain subsequent to June 6th, 1864, and to which as
Major he is not entitled, will be deducted in making payment under
this order.

*　　*　　*　　*　　*　　*　　*　　*

By command of Lieutenant-General Sheridan.

[Official.]　　　　　　　　　　R. C. DRUM, Adjutant-General.

(Signed) S. N. BENJAMIN, Assistant Adjutant-General.

Assistant Surgeon William C. Morrison. Resumed the practice
of his profession after his return from the service in 1865 at Cochranville, Chester County, Pa., where he continued in practice until
his health failed, about the year 1883. He declined rapidly, and
died of Bright's disease at the above place on February 19th, 1884,
and was buried at Faggs' Manor Burial Ground on Saturday, February 23d, aged 43 years.

Hospital Steward Reuben H. Smith, M. D. After the war
resumed the practice of medicine at Wilmington, Delaware, where
he remained until his health failed, early in 1882, when he came to
reside in West Chester with his son, Stephen T. Smith, until his
death, which took place March 6th, 1883, aged 71 years.

Principal Musician James St. John. Died in Philadelphia of
consumption, contracted from exposure in the service, on March
17th, 1868. He was buried in Lafayette Cemetery, Tenth and Fed-
eral Streets, Philadelphia.

CO. A.

First Lieutenant Frank C. Henry. Died at Coatesville February 26th, 1880.

Second Lieutenant Joseph Philips. Died.

John A. Groff. After having served as Recorder was elected
a Magistrate for the borough of West Chester, Pa., March 13th,
1877, and served until 1882.

21

Corporal Jacob Daubman. Died.
George M. Mintzer. Died.
Lewis Cochran. Died.
Joseph Edward Stott. Died January 13th, 1877.
James M. Haines. Erroneously reported dead, is living at Cedar Rapids, Iowa.
David M. Taylor. Was elected cashier of the Farmers' National Bank at Oxford, Chester County, Pa. He has continued to fulfill the duties of his responsible position with an honest fidelity and care, that in these days of financial crookedness and degeneracy on the part of so many high and trusted bank officials is most commendable.
Robert H. Humpton. Died.
Joseph E. Valentine. Immediately after his discharge from the service he entered upon preparation for the dental profession. He graduated with creditable success at the Pennsylvania College of Dental Surgery, in Philadelphia, in the class of 1867-68. He soon after located in the practice of his profession at Wilkesbarre, Luzerne County, Pa., where for several years he was successfully engaged. He now resides in Philadelphia, practicing his profession.
Jacob B. James. Died.
Edward O'Neil. Died.
Caleb Townsend. Died.
Andrew K. Wright. Died.

CO. B.

Captain Dallas Crow. Obtained a position in the money department of the Adams Express Company shortly after his discharge from the service. He has continued to receive the fullest confidence of the company. His duties are of the most responsible character, requiring not only accuracy and promptness, but the most sterling integrity.
Captain Jonas M. C. Savage. Has become disabled from his wounds received at Green Plains, Va., on May 18th, 1864, and is now an inmate of the Soldiers' Home at Hampton, Va.
First Lieutenant David S. Harry. Died.
George W. Wonderly. Died September 10th, 1873.

CO. C.

First Lieutenant Emmor G. Griffith. Was elected Assessor and Collector for the borough of West Chester in 1877, and served therein efficiently until elected Treasurer of Chester County in 1881. In these responsible positions he has performed the duties with fidelity and diligence, to the manifest advantage of both the borough and county. His term of office will expire with the present year.

Sergeant Isaac A. Cleaver. Was elected a director of the Penn Mutual Insurance Company and has served with much ability. He is actively engaged in mercantile business at Berwyn, in Easttown Township. He has been an active, enterprising citizen, energetic in the public welfare and its interests in his locality. He should become the successor in the State Legislature of his friend and neighbor, Captain William Wayne, the present member from that district.

Corporal Davis O. Taylor. Has pursued his vocation as machinist at West Chester since his discharge from the service. He has just received the nomination of his party for the office of Clerk of the Courts of Chester County, which, in a district polling an average majority of 2,300, is equivalent to an election. That he will bring to the discharge of the duties of the office the requisite ability and faithfulness, his record of service will fully justify the prediction.

William Agg. One of our badly wounded comrades. Received employment soon after the close of the war in the post-office department of Philadelphia. After some years of faithful service as a letter-carrier he was appointed to the charge of the sub-district of Kensington, where he continued to receive the confidence of the department until his death, which occurred after a short illness in 1883.

Anthony Grimes. Died in Philadelphia about 1878.

Levi Keeley. Died October 13th, 1864.

Asher M. Kinnard. Died at West Chester, of typhoid pneumonia, at 12 o'clock M., June 5th, 1883.

Wesley McLain. Erroneously reported dead, is still living at Milton, Northumberland County, Pa.

John L. Kitts. Received an appointment as paying teller in the National Bank of Delaware County, at which post he is still engaged.

CO. D.

Captain William S. Mendenhall. After the war settled in Wilmington, and was engaged in the retail notion and trimming trade. His health failed, resulting in consumption, of which he died at that place.

Sergeant William McCarty. Died.

Corporal Wilbur F. Flannery. Died of consumption at Pottstown, Pa., January 1st, 1879.

CO. E.

Sergeant Patrick Carter. Died.

John Bennett. Died March 25th, 1874.

Michael Walsh. Died of consumption at Concordville, May 24th, 1878.

CO. F.

Second Lieutenant Oliver E. Strickland. Died at home since the war.

Musician Thomas St. John. Died of consumption in Philadelphia, February 19th, 1880.

John Hall. Died.

George W. Wolf. Died in Philadelphia of consumption, November 4th, 1878.

Davis McAffee. Died July 12th, 1883, at his home in East Nantmeal, from the result of an operation necessitated by wounds received during the service.

CO. G.

John G. Herkins. Died of consumption, January, 1880.

Thomas L. Hinkson. Died in Philadelphia, February 27th, 1878.

CO. H.

Captain George A. LeMaistre. Has been engaged for several years as managing engineer for Walton, Whann & Co., manufacturers of phosphate — a most responsible position, requiring skill, accuracy and great care in the management of the details, to avoid the dangers attendant upon the chemical processes connected with the production and storage of large quantities of acids required in those works.

First Lieutenant Thomas S. Taylor. Was engaged after the war as a teacher of penmanship, for which he was very well qualified. He died of consumption at West Chester, 1883.

Sergeant Benjamin F. Smith. Died June 4th, 1872.

Sergeant Thomas John. Died at West Chester.

Corporal Isaac T. Massey. Died. Was killed by falling down stairs in Philadelphia on Christmas Day, 1878.

Jonathan Cross. Died.

Joseph Dasey. Died June 4th, 1872.

Milton Jackson. Died March 26th, 1876.

Edward H. Taylor. Died.

CO. I.

Second Lieutenant Annesley N. Morton. Died of pneumonia in Philadelphia, August 13th, 1880.

CO. K.

Captain William Wayne. Was elected a member of the House of Representatives of Pennsylvania in 1880; was re-elected in 1882, and has just received renomination for a third term in that body. His services as a member of the House need no other commendation than this repeated manifestation of confidence on the part of his constituents. As soldier and as statesman alike in faithfulness to the duties of the time, his presence with us here affords the opportunity to extend to him our hearty and united congratulations.

Captain William S. Underwood. Was elected in 1878 to the office of Register of Wills for Chester County, which position he filled with the same ability, fidelity and care that marked his services in the field. He is now the manager of an important business enterprise in the borough of West Chester.

Second Lieut. Marriott Brosius. Upon returning from the service entered Millersville State Normal School, from which he graduated. He was also a graduate of the Law Department of the University of Michigan. He afterwards studied law at Lancaster, Pa., with Hon. Thomas E. Franklin as his preceptor, and was admitted to practice at the Lancaster Bar in April, 1868. He has continued in the practice of his profession at Lancaster, with such diligence and careful attention to business as have brought to him an enviable success. In 1882 he was nominated by the Republican State Convention as Congressman-at-Large, but shared the defeat of his party in that election. He is a most eloquent and interesting speaker, whether in the political canvass or as a temperance advocate in its moral aspect, yet giving the cause the more practical advantage of his support of the party of progress, rather than follow the lead of merely theoretical and impracticable ideas of reform that tend to hinder and defeat the real purpose to be advanced. He has delivered many of the most interesting and eloquent Memorial Day addresses for the Grand Army of the Republic and other like ceremonies at various places; and to him has been assigned the duty of delivering the address upon this day of our Reunion, and I know that you will all be gratified in hearing the expression of his thoughts which these reminiscences of our old army days will give him the inspiration to speak to our ears and to our hearts.

Charles E. Raby. Died.

After the above had been read it was ascertained that the minutes of the association and the constitution and by-laws prepared for the action of this meeting had been inadvertently left at home by the secretary, who had gone to get them. This being stated by the president, on motion of Colonel Price, seconded by several comrades, it was decided to have the oration before concluding the business meeting. Colonel Guss then introduced our comrade, Hon. Marriott Brosius, who came forward, and was received with great applause. He then spoke as follows :

THE ORATION.

A more delightful task has rarely fallen to my hands than that which the partiality of your committee has assigned to me in connection with this Reunion; that of recalling some of the forgotten incidents, gathering up the fragrant recollections and patriotic reminiscences of our military career, and with a promethean spark from the altar of fraternal devotion, kindle them into new life until, like a restored picture, they appear in fresh brightness on the canvas of our memories to point the morals and illustrate the lessons of our service and our sacrifice.

The occasion, however, is not free from difficulty. Some of its aspects touch the heart in its tenderest part, and the mind is rather enfeebled than otherwise by the emotions which swell the breast, as the flood of affectionate remembrances and hallowed associations pour in ceaseless volume upon us, leaving little to the most earnest desire to discharge faithfully a delicate trust, but an acute sense of inability for the task. Still, we indulge the allurement of hope, that drawing inspiration from opportunity, we may be moved to some utterances that will tend to promote the reunion of this remnant of the old Regiment in the bonds of a firm and indissoluble friendship, and revive in our hearts the vestal flame of love for the memory of our comrades who suffered with us the parting, bore with us the burdens, won for us the victory, but came not back to share with us the glory.

My loving comrades, as we looked into each other's eyes to-day and touched each other's warm palms in fraternal greeting, memory, the soul's cup-bearer, brought back to us with great vividness the affecting incidents of our departure in November, 1861, when with hearts luminous with patriotic fire, with eyes flashing with brightness, with steps firm and true to the drum's tap, with a carriage which betrayed the fine pride and sturdy vigor of the young manhood which composed our rank and file, we marched through the streets of the borough, thronged with citizens and friends pressing eagerly to obtain a last embrace and a final farewell. Mothers with their cheeks suffused, and their faces mantled with a sweet sadness through which like a gleam of sunlight through a rift in the clouds flashed the great courage of their souls as they gave their sons with a mother's benediction to an imperilled country. Wives whose hearts were pierced by the unutterable grief of parting with those whose lives had been inseparably entwined with their own, stood like trembling vines from which the oak had been rudely torn, sustained by the unfaltering hope that a country saved would render back to the sweet embrace of love the dear offerings that day laid upon her altar. Sisters with their brows radiant with beauty, and their faces luminous with the glow of that divine sentiment which alone could make them capable of a deed so grand as when they bade their brothers with a God-speed to the scene of their duty, to brave the perils of the battle and the siege. Fathers whose hearts had been strengthened for the trial by the kindling fires of patriotism, stood grand and heroic as they consecrated with unbidden tears the gift of their boys to the cause of Union and liberty. And citizens in multitudes, all stirred alike by the awakening spirit of devotion which swept with electric touch, the heart-strings of a loyal people, greeted us with swaying hands, waving handkerchiefs and loud huzzas which culminated in enthusiastic shouts as the train bore us swiftly away. Who can contemplate the agonizing solicitude of that day, the pain of those partings, the anguish of those aching hearts, and the desolation of those broken homes, without feeling the uplifting touch of the sublime heroism of those who gave their first-born, and the splendid valor of those who went out in the early morning of their lives, a consecrated band, to keep watch at the gateway of the Union, as Gabriel and his band of holy angels kept their watch and walked the rounds of Paradise, willing if need be to gather into their own breasts the pittiless daggers of treason unsheathed for the nation's heart.

The occasion which summoned us from our homes and commanded our sacrifices will not lose its tragic interest while Americans enjoy the blessings, born to us out of the mighty scourge of civil war, which kindled the fires of death from Gettysburg to the Gulf. It seems to be the lesson of the ages that every new birth of freedom must have its dark night of travail and pain. Every marked advance in civilization has been made through fields of carnage. It has been through the Thermopylæs and over the Marathons and Gettysburgs of the world's history that civil and political liberty have carved their way to ultimate triumph. So our war was one of those overruling necessities in the providence of God in working out the destiny of the Republic. It was not for conquest or spoils. It was no rash and fruitless war for wanton glory waged. It was the spontaneous uprising of patriotism to rescue union and liberty, to establish and maintain the supremacy of ideas that will wander through eternity, principles as inextinguishable as the stars, and a civilization as shining as the sun.

Liberty and slavery—irreconcilable in their nature—crossed the ocean the same year. The Mayflower and the Dutch slave ship ploughed the sea at the same time. Both sought the shores of the New World and both planted their seeds to grow side by side until the principle of the survival of the fittest should exterminate one and nationalize the other. Formidable events in the history of their conflict put the nation to a formidable alternative—" the horrors of miasma or the fury of the blast." Said Victor Hugo: " For every oak struck by lightning, how many forests rendered wholesome." The storm came. Behind the visible work was the invisible, the latter sublime as the former was barbarous. Under a scaffolding of war was reared a majestic temple of human freedom. It was thus the character and magnitude of the undertaking which called us away, that signalized our departure as an event of no inconsiderable moment in the annals of Chester county. Then, too, many of the men who composed our Regiment were not those whom any community could afford to lose. Hundreds of homes surrendered to the recruiting officer their brightest and best. Young men of the highest character and most commanding talents abandoned the fields of employment for which they were conspicuously fitted by their superior character and intellectual equipment, and, turning their backs upon their dearly cherished hopes, took their places by the side of their comrades to swell the ranks of their country's defenders ; so that in the moral and intellectual character of its men, from the field to the rank and file, the Ninety-seventh had few superiors in the service ; and the people, not alone those who endured the heart pangs of separation and loss, but the whole community, instinctively felt a sense of impending calamity as they witnessed the departure of the flower of their young manhood.

To adjust ourselves to our new relations and become as capable in our new field of operations as we had been efficient in the less exciting pursuits of peace was an undertaking whose difficulties the uninitiated cannot easily appreciate. A good soldier is a machine. He moves at the word of command, as the shuttle flies at the touch

of a spring. Intelligence and judgment as agencies in the direction
of individual movement have little place in the principles and rules
of military organization and discipline ; and a man who has been accustomed to turning to the right or left, or advancing in a straight
line at his own will, surrenders a large share of his personal liberty
when he consents to go forward or turn aside at the command of
another. One accustomed to express his opinion freely in season and
out of season, with knowledge and without knowledge, makes a sad
and melancholy sacrifice of his freedom of speech when he consents
to hold his tongue except when permitted to speak. Some of us were
dull scholars in this despotic school of military limitations upon human rights, and sometimes embarrassments ensued upon an undue
assertion of that deeply cherished right to speak our mind. Comrade
Miles, of Company E, thought the propriety of holding Jacksonville
was a question upon which every citizen and soldier as well, had a
right to an opinion, and when preparations for evacuation were being
made and he accidentally met General Wright, he saw no harm in
remarking to him, " General, I thought you would have to '*vaceate*,' "
and we can imagine his surprise when his temerity was rewarded by
an order for an escort to conduct him to private quarters. But this
surrender of individual liberty ; this complete subjection to the dominion of arbitrary rule, was not a badge of degrading servitude, but
a high and patriotic duty, and a part of the voluntary sacrifice the
citizen made when he became a soldier. And hard as it was at times
to brook this submission when our own judgment rose in hot revolt
against a command, the reason for which was not discoverable, while
its inutility and danger were apparent to all, yet no disobedience or
even reluctance, to respond to the command of a superior ever im-
paired the efficiency of the Ninety-seventh. Our fighting qualities
were never at a discount, and we fairly earned the compliments ex-
torted from casual observers of our steadfast courage and invincible
prowess. It was an aid of one of the Generals who, witnessing our
dauntless bravery and obstinate courage as we held the line under a
tempest of fire at Foster's Place, on the 18th of May, '64, remarked,
" The Ninety-seventh will hold that line for three weeks if they are
supplied with ammunition." It reminds us of the brave Colonel
George of a Minnesota regiment at the battle of Chickamauga, who
promised still better. When an aid came with the inquiry as to how
long his regiment could hold a certain pass, he sent back the heroic
answer, " Till we are mustered out." So at the Darbytown road ; an
officer who witnessed our splendid and successful charge said to

Colonel Pennypacker, " That's the d——st regiment of yours to fight I ever saw ! " He was informed by the Colonel that it was the result of early training, but I think something was due to inherited qualities—courage in the blood, and it illustrated what every machinist knows, the better the material, the better the machine. But in displaying these high qualities of the soldier we were only being true to ourselves. Obedience, subordination, devotion and courage were all comprised in that first great self-imposed command, " Go ye and serve your country until Union and Liberty are rescued from the despoiler's hands."

That our boys behaved so well may be due in part to the fact that for a long time they were under a mother's watchful eye. Boys will put their best foot foremost when mother is looking on. A noble woman, like the King's name in battle, is a mighty incentive. Mrs. Mary St. John (I would rather call her St. Mary John) exerted an elevating and beneficent influence upon all who came within her radiant ministry of kindness and helpfulness. She did not lead in battle like Joan of Arc, or command a fortress like Lady Banks, or fire the cannon like Molly Pitcher ; but she was behind us :

"In danger, mind you, a woman behind you
Can turn your blood to fire."

The gentle sway of her womanly scepter, her self-sacrifice, devotion and tender care, followed the battle, like the sunshine the storm, alleviating pain, assuaging the distresses of sickness and smoothing the wrinkled brow of the soldier's life. O, woman !

"When pain and anguish wring the brow,
A ministering angel thou."

Mother St. John brought into the camp something of the influence of home. Gen. Sherman used to say that the home influences were of infinite assistance in the dicipline of the army. It was a benediction to any regiment to enjoy the presence and be subject to the dominion of a woman's influence, and so profoundly sensible are we of the value of her association with the regiment, so fragrant is our recollection of her tender and affectionate care, that I know I but voice the spontaneous emotion of every heart when I invoke blessings upon Mother St. John. May time deal with her gently, may the days of her years be lengthened out, and joy and happiness be the companions of her age.

The services of the regiment during an exceptionally checkered career of good and bad fortune comprised every variety of experience possible to military life. We fought rebels and likewise malaria and mosquitoes. We measured swords with the enemies of our country on many a well-contested field; we wrestled manfully with the enemies of our constitutions in the form of southern fevers that walked in the darkness and stalked abroad at noonday : and we had many sanguinary encounters with the winged and venomous disturbers of our comfort and peace that marshalled their hosts in every swamp, assailed every out-post and invaded every camp on the southern coast with malign and ravenous intent to feast with rancorous rapture on the sweet and nourishing blood of the North. We were wood choppers on Sea Brook, lumbermen on the St. Mary's, dock builders at Port Royal, sappers on Morris Island, engineers on Hilton Head, and miners at Petersburg. Our reveille and tattoo sounded in every degree of latitude from Washington to St. Augustine. Our camp-fires blazed in every coast state from Maryland to Florida. Our victorious eagles were borne from Hampton Roads to Port Royal ; from Pulaski to Jacksonville ; from Fernandina to Morris' Island ; from the rice swamps of the Carolinas to the trenches of the Peninsula. Our wild hurrahs rang out and our avenging bayonets gleamed from the slopes of Wagner, Gregg and Fisher. We forced the gates of Wilmington, unfurled our battle-scarred flag in the streets of Goldsboro, and swinging to the capital of the State, we stood in its shadow, proud spectators of a glorious triumph, as the last army of the "Confederacy" laid its arms at the feet of Sherman's conquering legions, and the curtain fell before the tragedy of the rebellion.

In contemplating the career of our regiment, we cannot over-look the melancholy shadows which form the sombre background for the more cheerful and exhilarating incidents of our diversified experience. We cannot look into each others' eyes to-day without being reminded of our unreturning comrades who are bivouacked under eternal skies on the plains beyond the river. It was a solemn hour when we stood beside our first grave and endured the pangs of our first grief. Every family has its first death ; we had ours when comrade Stevens, of Co. F., in January, 1862, closed his loyal service to his country and was mustered out. He but led the way, for our death roll was long and illustrious. The noble and gifted Hambleton ; the gentle and studious Gardner ; the sturdy and faithful Taylor ; the vigorous and manly Brinton ; the brave and impetuous Hawkins ; the brilliant and daring Carruthers, and the young and gallant Morton, but represent the harvest of death gathered from our line, and rank and file, and suggest the splendid aggregate of purity, patriotism, intellect, devotion and all the high qualities of manhood that swelled the sacrifice which the Ninety-seventh laid upon our country's bleeding altar.

How can we fitly honor the memory of our valiant dead? Let us dwell for a moment upon their patriotic services and meritorious death. I have great faith in the influence upon the living of the remembrances of the heroic dead. It was such an influence that led a young Greek two thousand years ago, when walking over the fields on which a Grecian warrior won his victories, to exclaim : "the trophies of Miltiades will not let me sleep." So with the contemplation of the sacrifices and splendid courage of our departed comrades, may come an incantation that will conjure spirits of high patriotism round about us, until like Hector's son we catch heroic fire from the memory of the tried fidelity and steadfast devotion of our fallen braves.

Vain are the eulogies of the living upon the noble men whom the tide of battle and its allied destroyer, fell disease, swept to the skies from camp and field. They were soldiers in the most exalted sense. Their helmets were of faith, their breastplates were of courage, their swords were of justice. They entered the war in something of the spirit of Gustavus of Sweden, at Lutzen, when spurning his corselets he exclaimed "God is my harness." Our boys went into battle inspired with all the heroism of the Revolution. They marched into the fight with Wayne and all the heroes of Brandywine, Paoli and Valley Forge, in the air above them. The typical bravery of the Union soldier was well exemplified by an incident told of Gen. Dan McCook. He was storming the heights of Kenesaw Mountain at the head of his troops. The summit was crowded with rebel soldiers ; the ascent was precipitous ; the troops had to lift themselves up by the bushes and branches of the trees ; he knew it was certain death. In a momentary pause in the ascent he was heard to repeat, in calm, clear tones, these lines from Macaulay's Lays of Ancient Rome :

"Then out spoke brave Horatius, the captain of the gate,
To every man upon this earth death cometh soon or late,
And how can man die better than by facing fearful odds
For the ashes of his fathers and the temples of his gods?

A moment afterwards he rushed up the heights, and in two minutes fell dead "for the ashes of his fathers and the temples of his gods." The same spirit animated and inspired our men in many a perilous encounter. On Morris Island, the night of Wagner's evacuation, when our line was formed for the advance, the glittering sentinels of heaven—the watching stars—witnessing our impatience for the assault, our dauntless Major, whose breast was glowing with the foreshining of the glory of the anticipated achievement, addressing the regiment, said: " Men, remember your duty to God and your country to-night." The thrilling words went down the line like an electric pulse, touching off a magazine of heroic daring in every heart, in the blaze of which every man would have scaled the walls of Wagner, pikes, lances and all, or found a grave in the attempt. There are times when the soldier seems transformed; swept on by the wings of the tempest of excitement; riding on the billows of impetuous heroism; insensible to danger, knowing no fear, he is more than man. We have seen our boys marching into the jaws of death with as firm and steady a step as they would pursue the commonest paths of life. At Green Plains they charged against a hurricane of fire before which none but lines of adamant could stand. O, mortal powers, what courage! How like gods they moved, yet how like men they fell, these citizen soldiers, many of whom but the week before had left their kisses on the lips of mothers, wives and sisters in exchange for their benedictions, as they rushed to their baptism of fire! But how could they die better? Near the beginning of the century a great battle was fought on the plains of the Danube, resulting in a victory for France. The courage of a private soldier contributed to the triumph, and ever after, at the parades of the battalion, the name of Latour D'Vergne was first called, when the eldest sergeant stepped to the front and answered, " died on the field of honor." So in Walhalla, the paradise of battle-scarred warriors, when on the roll of heroes the names of our martyred comrades are called, a chorus of dauntless spirits will reverberate along the celestial corridors as the highest eulogy is pronounced, "died on the field of duty." To their character our praise can add nothing; not to their valor, for that is immortal; not to their patriotism, for that is in the Recording Angel's book; not to their sublime endurance, for that is embalmed in history's page. Helpless to add a single flower to the immortal wreathes that must forever crown their immortal deeds, we can but resign them to their rest with the prayer of Chester County's sweet poet on the field of Gettysburg:

" Take them, O, Fatherland,
Who, dying, conquered in Thy name!
Take them, O, God, our brave,
The glad fulfilment of Thy dread decree!
Who grasped the sword for peace, and smote to save,
And dying here for freedom, died for Thee."

Thus have our dead completed their task; but ours, my comrades, remains unfinished. The nation's martyrs left as a legacy to their surviving countrymen the best government ever devised by human wisdom for the happiness of mankind, and as we recall their sacrifices that government of the people, by the people and for the people might not perish from the earth, is it irreverent to believe that our dead, who from camp and field went up to God in the shadow of our flag and who still love their country, are assembled with us to-day in their viewless forms, and with their celestial voices are dedicating their surviving comrades to the holy ministry of preserving for all coming time what they died to save. This is our unfinished task. Let us for a moment consider the commanding duties it lays upon us.

"The walls of my city," said an ancient ruler, "are the hearts of my people." So the surest defences of this Republic are the hearts of its citizens, when imbued with an intelligent sense of the responsibilities and a loyal devotion to the obligations of citizenship. If there is one overruling necessity, one fundamentally essential factor in the true solution of the problem of our destiny, it is a standard of moral independence, political integrity, obedience and loyalty, that will guarantee a citizenship at once independent, incorruptible, obedient to law and loyal to the public weal. So this Republic with a voice of solemn supplication, emphasized by the sacrifices of the past, summons the manhood on which it leans to-day to lift itself up to the true stature of American citizenship.

Without a vigorous, noble and true manhood, though our empire reach from sea to sea, we are a rope of sand. The French king was not wholly wrong when he said "I am the State." He was part of it. Not one man, but all men, are the State.

"Not high raised battlements or labored mounds, thick wall nor moated gate,
Nor cities proud with spires and turrets crowned, nor starred and spangled courts,
Where low-born baseness wafts perfume to pride, but men, high-minded men,
Who their duties know, but know their rights and knowing, dare maintain."

Seek ye, then, first intelligence, virtue, honor, independence and loyalty to principle in the citizen, and all the blessings of good government will be added unto you. Fidelity to conviction, devotion to duty, loyalty to conscience and country, are the qualities which moulded the men who honored American citizenship and adorned the public service in the past, and it is a hope in aid of whose realization all the graves filled by our civil war implore the living, that the influence of American civilization and the inspiration of American progress may produce for Columbia's future citizens a race of men who, " being admirable in form, noble in reason, infinite in faculty," will add thereto integrity of soul—a mighty priesthood of truth, who will barter not their honor at the public marts, stock boards, election polls or in halls of legislation, but will stand with manly firmness against all the blandishments of power and the seductions of ambition and gold, as integrity incarnate.

The infirmities common to forms of government in which sovereignty resides in the people and speaks through popular elections have their roots in individual delinquency and personal venality. The seeds of political degeneracy lurk in that condition of personal character which makes it possible for men to violate the plainest requirements of morality to advance a political end. It is a low standard of character, an enfeebled moral sense, insensibility to the stain of dishonor in the voter, that nurtures the poisonous tree of political evil and hurries it on to its tainted bloom and deadly fruitage.

In the breast of the voter is the virus that taints the blood of our political life, and the decay of character is the unerring prelude to degeneracy in our political institutions.

"Ill fares the land, to hastening ills a prey,
Where wealth accumulates and men decay."

The evils sometimes betrayed in political administration, the corruption which the tumultuous heaving of popular elections sometimes throws to the surface, are but the hectic flush on the cheek of the body politic which betrays the existence of the subtle poison of moral decay, consuming its life. We are without hope of preserving the lofty character which the splendor of our history has won for us unless we can keep upright the hearts of our people and pure the homes of the land, thereby maintaining a perennial supply of high-minded men who, like our martyred Lincoln, can be statesmen without craftiness, and politicians without intrigue, who can subject their political conduct to the restraints of moral principle, and subordinate their private interests to their public duties ; whose chastity of honor and sensibility of principle make them feel the sense of delinquency or the stain of dishonor as a wound, and who, like the virtuous Andrew Fletcher, would give their lives to serve their country, but would not do a base thing to save it.

The people are the source of authority, the fountain of power, the keepers of the Republic's jewels. Whatever measure of virtue, self-restraint, patriotism and honor shall exalt them, in that same measure will their collective action feel the uplifting touch. As they shall think, and feel, and act, so shall be formed and directed the mightiest engine of power the world has ever known, whose mandates kings and potentates obey, and at whose touch governments are dismantled and dynasties dissolved, the sovereign of all earthly powers—public sentiment—an exalted assemblage, it has been said, which without visible session, ever legislates, and without army or navy, marshal or constable, ever executes its decrees. Remove the atmosphere from the earth, said a philosopher, and all the water would fly into vapor. Public sentiment is the atmosphere of society, without which our institutions would fly into chaos; and unless that atmosphere is pure and wholesome the body politic cannot be healthy. The vicious sentiments and depraved morals of the individual diffuse themselves and impair the tone of the social and political atmosphere, as the polluted breath of the sot taints the air around him. This all-encasing air, the very breath of life to our political existence, must be kept from pollution if we hope to preserve our free institutions from decay and ultimate dissolution.

A nation of fifty millions cannot be saved by the virtuous remnant, but the infirmities of the majority must be healed. Moral health must inhabit, and political soundness invigorate the whole body; for Matthew Arnold is right, as Plato and the prophets were right before him, that where the majority are bad, the minority cannot lead to the promised land, but the supremacy of the true, the just, the pure and elevated will as certainly redeem and save the nation, as the dominion of their opposites, by an inexorable fatality, will destroy it.

That which righteousness exalts, sin destroys. What virtue, honor, loyalty and loving duty adorn and strengthen, vice, neglect, intrigue and profligacy enfeeble and despoil. Indifference, selfishness, venality and every insidious device to obstruct the sovereign will are as fatal as the breath of the sirocco to the fair gardens of our political heritage. The few can carry wrong results, promote vicious policies, advance dangerous principles and elevate corrupt men, only when the many sleep upon their rights. Demagogues are powerless to harm when the people are vigilant to save. But if the voters give themselves up to indolent indifference to the results of the primary organization of political power, and suffer the collective action to be moulded and declared by the least qualified in intelligence, principle

and probity ; if they are content to abandon the sources of political
action to the venal, the stupid and the servile, it becomes as certain
as the fiat of omnipotence that the country will express and obey the
baser will, the supremacy of patriotism and public reason be over-
thrown, while faction, ambition, selfishness and corruption will sit
regnant in the seat of power.

Hence it is, to be false to the cardinal virtues which enter into
the structure of a man, adorning and strengthening his character ; a
conscious rectitude which inspires him with self-respect and gives
him the courage, consequence and stateliness born of self-regard ; an
intelligence and patriotism, which qualify him to judge, stimulate his
exertions, and hold him in steadfast loyalty to his country's needs ;
and an independence which enables him to stand four square to all
the winds that blow ; to be recreant to these conspicuous attributes
of a good citizen is disloyalty to the memory of our martyred comrades and treason to the Republic. Shall it be in vain, then, that we
plead for the elevation of the citizen—for a vigorous and virtuous
manhood—for high-minded and true-hearted men who alone can
save this country from a disappointed hope and a blighted destiny ?
The glory of the Republic is her manhood, and when that becomes
debased, the sand in the hour-glass of her history will begin to run.
And I desire to add, my comrades, that if the time shall come when
the Republic, which we devoutly pray the God of nations may preserve to be the Union soldiers' temple of fame, falls a victim to maladies
engendered in the bosom of our political system, when corruption
shall have eaten away the cable that holds us to the moorings of virtue ; "when the nation shall totter to its fall, its glory extinct, the
banner of its pride trampled in the dust, its nationality and grandeur
a moral of history," when the unfriendly prophecy of a hundred
years ago shall be fulfilled, and a few lean and half naked fishermen
are dividing with owls and foxes the ruins of our great cities, wash-
ing their nets amid the relics of our gigantic docks and building their
huts out of the capitals of our stately edifices, let not this work of
ruin be traced to those who wore the Union blue. We are a consecrated band. It was at the battle of Chickamauga, just after a vigorous assault of the enemy had been gallantly repulsed at the point
of the bayonet that the great-hearted commander, George H. Thomas,
took the hand of a private soldier and thanked him for his courage. The soldier stood silent a moment, and then said with emotion : "George H. Thomas has taken this hand in his ; I'll knock
down any mean man that offers to take it hereafter." He felt that

something had consecrated his hand, making it too sacred for vulgar touch. Comrades, something has consecrated every surviving soldier of the Union. No man that drew a sword or carried a musket in that holy war, or bore our battle-stained banner on any one of the glorious fields on which the Union arms won imperishable renown, but is solemnly dedicated to the service of patriotism, honor, loyalty and virtue, to the end that the soldiery that once saved the nation by fire and sword may save it yet again by the example of their fidelity to the principles and institutions of the government.

After Appomattox General Lee made the great speech of his life, when he said to his vanquished army, "Soldiers! we have done our duty, as we knew it, now let us go home and be good citizens."

A greater than Lee, the nation's silent chieftain also spoke, and his utterance will not soon die—"Let us have peace!" One is the fruit of the other, and the prayer of the Republic to-day is that we be good citizens and enjoy the blessings of peace and concord. From the hearts of patriots everywhere, attuned to the same melody, is lifted up the glad refrain ; celestial choirs prolong the joyful chorus until the spirits of our martyred dead send back the swelling anthem, " Let us be good citizens,"—" Let us have peace."

The maintenance of this lofty standard of personal character and exalted patriotism in the citizen ; the enthronement in our public life of unselfish loyalty and disinterested devotion to duty, and the establishment of the dominion of incorruptible integrity and stainless honor as the predominant spirit in the public service of the country is the elevated task to which patriotism dedicates American citizenship. My Comrades! do we realize the responsibility of the task imposed? Are we equal to this supreme demand? Are we fit for this exalted service? These are the questions which the sphinx of national destiny puts to us, on the inexorable condition of death if not correctly answered. But if the patriotism of the American people, putting under its feet sectional animosity, partisan bitterness, factious dissension, personal and political profligacy, selfishness and all uncharitableness, shall bear back to us on unflagging wing the answer yea! yea! then will the American Republic stand a monument to the memory of the heroic sacrifices of its citizens, when the pyramids are not, and Karnak is forgotten.

Comrades, I have indulged these reflections because they point the way to the honorable completion of our yet unfinished task ; because I feel the elevating influence of these high ideals ; because I believe there are spirit hands reaching down to-day to clasp ours of

flesh in token of continued fellowship in the promotion of that purity
of life and elevation of character which alone can qualify the nation
for the splendid career and exalted destiny that await it.

Animated by these views and inspired by these hopes, Americans can hold fast their faith that the young Republic of the West,
moving in queenly majesty in the procession of the nations ; proudly
eminent; guided by principles which follow in the wake of Christi-
anity as verdure follows the path of the sun ; freighted with the gold-
en triumphs of the past ; the heir of all the ages, and led by faith in
an immortal destiny as by a pillar of cloud by day and of fire by
night, will continue her march down the centuries, plucking new
laurels and winning new victories for man and government, until
ripe with years and with a completed destiny she lays the finished
crown of her glory at the feet of Jehovah, at the jubilee of eternity.

During the entire delivery of the address the most perfect
attention was given by the men, standing in solid mass around the
platform before the speaker, whose eloquence and impressive words
imparted their influence upon all. Applause was frequently given
to some of the stirring sentiments. At the conclusion most hearty
cheers were given the orator.

Sergeant Isaac A. Cleaver moved a vote of thanks for the able,
interesting and eloquent address of Comrade Brosius, which no
words of ours could adequately convey, save by the feeling within
our hearts which responded to its eloquent utterances. The motion
was seconded by Captain George A. Lemaistre, Co. H, and Colonel
John Wainwright, and was passed unanimously by the voice of
every comrade present in response.

David M. Taylor of Co. A then presented the following resolutions :

WHEREAS, The expense incurred by Colonel Price in publishing
the History of the Ninety-seventh Regiment, Pennsylvania Volunteers, still exceeds by $300 the amount yet realized from the sale of
books ; and

WHEREAS, It seems right and proper that the author of this
valuable historic record of the members and the services of the
Regiment should be relieved of this indebtedness ; therefore

Resolved, That we, the surviving members, assembled at the
Reunion of the Regiment this 29th day of October, 1884, hereby
authorize and direct the treasurer of our association to pay over to

Brevet-Cr nel Isaiah Price $300, and receive therefor sixty copies of the H.. .ory.

Resolved, That the president shall appoint a committee of five, whose duty shall be to take charge of said Histories and sell the same as opportunity may offer, the proceeds accruing therefrom to be paid into the treasury at the annual meeting. Said committee to have full discretionary power to *present* copies to *worthy members* and the *families of deceased members* who are unable to purchase them.

Before the question upon the resolutions was taken Colonel Price said, he desired to say that this action was a surprise to him, and entirely without his concurrence; that he only asked of the members of the Regiment such individual subscriptions as might be desired by them. But if the association intended to procure the number of books named in the resolutions, he could only say the books were on hand.

Sergeant Cleaver then stated that while in feeling he had the most hearty concurrence in the object of the resolutions to reimburse Colonel Price for the unliquidated balance of cost for publishing the History, it was necessary for the members of the association to know that, if these resolutions were passed, there was not sufficient funds in the treasury to meet the amount named, and it was a question yet undemonstrated whether the association would be in a condition to meet such an order as at present constituted, and referred to the general expenses for this Reunion, which would perhaps exhaust the treasury of its present provision for funds.

Colonel Price then asked that the mover of the resolutions should consent to withdraw them, which, after some further remarks by Comrade Taylor and others, was done by him.

The secretary, Major L. R. Thomas, having now returned with the minutes and other papers, they were read by him as presented in the foregoing account of the meeting of May 3d.

On motion the minutes were adopted as read.

The chairman, Colonel Guss, then stated the first business in order to be an election of officers to serve for the coming year.

On motion of Marriott Brosius, Esq., the present officers were re-elected for another year.

As the chairman, upon whom, in accordance with the by-laws, the duty devolved of calling the association together, desired to have some expression from the comrades present as to their wishes in the matter, the question of how often it was best to have future Reunions of the association was then taken up. Various suggestions were made by different comrades as to time, varying from one to five years.

Captain W. James, Co. G, moved that the Reunions be annually.

D. M. Taylor, Co. A, favored less frequent meetings, on account of many having to come from long distances and at considerable expense.

Sergeant Cleaver also referred to the difficulties attending these gatherings, many of the comrades not being in such financial condition as to bear the expense.

Dr. Worrall, Co. B, was urgent in the support of an annual Reunion. He said we were growing older each year, and Colonel Guss, was not the only white head here to-day, and our numbers are growing less every year. Five years is a long time, and some of us may not be living to assemble at the next if it be so long deferred. Let us meet together each year and touch elbows again as of yore, and enjoy our life while we live in reviving these old memories, and let our association keep us warmly united in feeling and interest. We can all afford to come together one day in each year and be boys again, and renew our soldier life, as now we are inspired by mingling in social intercourse with each other.

Several motions were suggested, proposing two, three and five years. But the question upon the motion of Captain James being seconded, was first taken up, and decided in the affirmative almost unanimously.

The date for holding the meeting being now the subject for consideration, the 29th of October was first mentioned by Colonel Guss as one as appropriate as any in consequence of its being the time of our organization, but as the weather was liable to be cold, and perhaps stormy, it might be well to fix upon an earlier day.

Colonel Price suggested the 11th of September, as that was about the time of the first occupation of Camp Wayne; or the 22d of August, the date of the muster-in of Co. A, the first company of the Regiment organized. After considerable expressions by Comrades Brosius, Cleaver, Captain James, Dr. Worrall, Colonel Guss, Colonel Lewis, D. M. Taylor, Co. A, Sergeant McBride, Co. D, Sergeant Kent, Co. C, and others, on motion of Sergeant Cleaver it was decided to hold the next Reunion on the third Wednesday in August, and in West Chester as the most available and central place for these occasions.

Colonel Guss then declared the business meeting closed, and

asked the comrades to get their dinner tickets and meet in the hall for the banquet.

Before separating Colonel Price announced that Mr. Marshall, photographer of West Chester, was in readiness on the ground to take a photographic group of the Regiment, and asked the comrades to take position before the camera on the right of the stand. With ready promptness of movement the entire body of men stood side by side in solid mass before the camera, as, in times gone by, they had stood shoulder to shoulder under arms, looking into the cannon's mouth unquailingly at Wagner, Gregg and Sumter; before Petersburg and Richmond; at Cold Harbor, at Fort Harrison, at Fort Fisher and the gates of Wilmington. With these experiences engraven upon their bronzed faces, they could calmly look into the milder mouth of the camera about to be opened upon their defenseless faces without fear of the consequences. At such a moment Mr. Marshall could not have found a more fitting and appropriate suggestion than that he made, " Perhaps you had better take off your hats." Little could he know the instant feeling of every soldier there of the suggestive contrast conveyed by his words. To *us* it brought back again the cry of the " Lookout! " " Wagner, cover! " " Johnson, cover! " when with bated breath we awaited the result of the impending "whang bang" of the shell as it exploded over our devoted heads.

Two seconds sufficed for the first shot from the camera, when Mr. Marshall requested a few minutes to prepare for a second assault, which was as unflinchingly faced.

Then the word of command was given to move upon the works within the Exhibition Hall. The charge was short, sharp and decisive, and the citadel occupied by the voracious invaders within less time than it takes to recite the particulars.

The tables, ten or twelve in number, were found to be well provided with all that the hunger, or the fastidious taste, could desire, showing that the committee in charge of this most important part of the arrangements well understood the requirements of the situation ; for had they not with them all the experience of the importance of the Commissary and Quartermaster Departments being placed in capable and competent hands? And with this knowledge of a soldier's expectations they were sure to have the rations well up to the front when the halt was called, and the camp kettles were to be rattled out of the baggage trains ready for instant service.

The committee of arrangements had decorated the building in

most admirable taste with a profusion of bunting that called forth the admiration of all, and the presence of the old emblems of our service stirred the patriotic heart of every veteran present.

When all had taken their places at the tables, the central one being occupied by Colonel Guss at the head, with Mother St. John and her daughter on his right; with the orator of the day, Lieutenant Brosius, Colonels Wainwright and Price and Captain Wayne on his left, and opposite to him our veteran Chaplain, whose first experience of leading the religious services in camp was in front of Petersburg, at brigade headquarters, the Sunday after his arrival at the front, when in the midst of the prayer a shell from the rebel batteries broke just overhead and scattered its fragments in the midst of the congregation, and wounded a man at his side. Undismayed by what might well make an old soldier seek cover, he stuck it out and finished the invocation, no doubt feeling in his heart he was seeking the best refuge for man in any emergency. So we may say "our veteran Chaplain," was then called upon by Colonel Guss to ask the Divine blessing upon our repast, which he did in a few well-chosen words.

The following programme and bill of fare, prepared by the committee, had been circulated among the comrades previous to the meeting:

REUNION

OF

NINETY-SEVENTH REGIMENT, P. V.,

WEST CHESTER, PA.,

WEDNESDAY, OCTOBER 29TH, 1884.

ORDER OF EXERCISES.

MEET AT FAIR GROUNDS,	II A. M.
BUSINESS MEETING,	II A. M. TO 12 M.
ORATION (COMRADE MARRIOTT BROSIUS),	12 A. M.
DINNER,	1.30 P. M.

BILL OF FARE.

ROASTS.

BEEF.   LAMB.   TURKEY.

BREAD.   ROLLS.   BUTTER.

CHICKEN SALAD.   OYSTERS ON SHELL.

CRANBERRY SAUCE.   CELERY.

CHOWCHOW.   MIXED PICKLES.

SPANISH OLIVES.   WORCESTERSHIRE SAUCE.   MUSTARD.

COFFEE.

FRUITS.

APPLES.   GRAPES.   BANANAS.

ICE CREAM.

VANILLA.   CHOCOLATE.

MIXED CAKES.

Then the replenishment of the inner man was commenced, in order that "the feast of reason and flow of soul" might receive the fuller inspiration of the thankful hearts thus gathered together here once more in cordial and fraternal association, partaking joyously again of the bountiful gifts provided for the sustenance of life and for the growth of our common natures into even more and more perfect harmoniousness of intercourse in all the varied relations of life.

What other class of our people could have a higher or better appreciation of such a meeting as this between the comrades of the war thus gathered to perpetuate the memories of their toils and sacrifices encountered in the line of duty which caused the loss of so many lives of our comrades whom we sadly miss at a time like this, when we realize so keenly the vacant place at our side once filled by loved comrades whose last answer to the roll-call was long ago, just before the battles at Foster's, Green Plains, Fort Fisher, Drury's Bluff, or others that we remember as these?

During the repast, Wilson's Orchestra discoursed most excellent music, which enlivened the spirits of all as they partook of the viands set before them.

When at length the siege of the tables had resulted in the demolition of the more than abundant supplies provided, and the sense of renewed content of body and mind began to be manifest, the president, Colonel H. R. Guss, rapped for order, and called attention to the next business as arranged upon the programme by the committee, which was the regular toasts prepared for this occasion. The reading of these was then proceeded with in the following order :

FIRST REGULAR TOAST.

"The Citizen Soldier. When baptized in the fire of battle became the Veteran."

> " Corporal Casey, can't you be aisy ?
> Your gun is on my foot.
> If you can't ground arms without such harms
> You shall be the captain's cook."

Colonel D. W. C. Lewis was named for this toast, and responded as follows :

The citizen soldier! Name honored by sage and poet! Let memory carry you back to the winter of '60 and '61, when we were all engaged in pursuits of peace and industry—the farmer at his plow, the mechanic in his shop, the merchant at his business and the student at his studies—without a thought of what was to follow in the near future. The muttering and threats of treason began to be heard in the North, borne by every breeze that came from the sunny South. As insult after insult was hurled by traitors, at the government and the flag of our country, our blood began to boil, and we listened with bated breath and waited patiently for the time to come when we could strike under the laws, for the laws and by the laws for our country and its laws.

That time soon came. On the 15th of April, 1861, there came flashing over the wires the news of the firing upon and capture of Fort Sumter, followed by a call from that prince of Presidents, Abraham Lincoln, for seventy-five thousand men to help him enforce the law that bore so lightly on all. You all remember how that call was obeyed. In less than twenty-four hours the men who, up to that time, had been engaged in pursuits of peace and industry, responded in more than thrice the number of the call, transformed and enrolled as citizen soldiers, sworn to defend and, if need be, die in defence of their country.

How were these obligations kept? Consult history and see what the citizen soldiers have undergone in defence of their country and for the purpose of perpetuating their love of liberty and free thought. Their graves mark hillside and valley from Maine to Mexico, from Atlantic's shore to Rocky Mountain slope. Their wounded and suffering ones are in your midst. The people should not forget them—they whose whitened heads show that they are blossoming for the grave. But remember that they are but a part of the grand army of citizen soldiers who gave their all to save the Republic.

You all remember Sixty-one,
When crime and treason had begun
To agitate our happy land.
With one accord a patriot band,
For freedom's defence, both good and grand,
With trust in powder, faith in God,
They were at best an awkward squad.

But years roll by. This squad you find
On battle front and picket line,
'Mid bristling bayonet, shot and shell,
Sulphurous smoke and fumes of hell,
Union cheers and rebel yell,
Where they by scores and hundreds fell
In the great, grand cause
For freedom, country and the laws,
Quick to avenge, would no insult brook,
Felt it no disgrace "to be captain's cook."

"Woman! Without her the world would be empty, fruitless."

> "Men are what women make them; age and youth
> Bear witness to that grand eternal truth;
> They steer the bark o'er destiny's dark wave,
> And guide us from the cradle to the grave."

To this toast Colonel Isaiah Price was called upon to answer.

My Comrades: I regard it an especial honor to have been invited to respond to this toast upon the occasion of this Reunion, here in this familiar place, which we all remember so well. For here it was that our first experiences of a soldier's life and duty were begun, ere yet the separation from our homes and loved ones had sharpened into the keenness of our later sense of the privations, the toils, the dangers and those sterner realities of war so soon to be encountered, which were then so dimly perceived, so little realized, amid the busy stir and throng of preparation that preceded our going forth.

Perhaps this unconsciousness of what was to be experienced was mainly due to the presence here in our first camp, of those best helpmates of life in every emergency, the devoted mothers, wives, sisters and daughters, who—thrusting back the agony and the tears that gnawed within their hearts and dimmed their eyes through the torturing fears born of their love for sons, husbands, brothers and fathers going forth to battle—gathered about us here in those days of solemn preparation, and sought to nerve our hearts to fortitude and duty through the ministration of their hands, bringing the profusion of supplies for our comfort in camp and field ; seeking through every tender influence of loving interest to beguile the pangs of parting ; enforcing the smiles that could not quite conceal the traces of the deeper anguish of heart, that must be hushed with more than Spartan effort as the hour of our departure drew nigh.

Ah! those were truly deserving of being counted "heroic women" who, twenty-three years ago this October day, illustrated anew the noblest, truest womanhood for the age in which they lived.

We read of "Spartan mothers" who bade their sons go forth in the defence of their country in the hour of danger, and who held up their babes to behold the departure of their fathers to do battle for their homes.

History has immortalized the women of Greece who devoted themselves to the rescue of their country from the grasp of the invader. Veturia and Volumnia are remembered for their devotion and self-sacrifice that saved Rome from the vengeance of their banished son and husband.

The name of Joan of Arc will enkindle the flame of patriotic enthusiasm so long as time shall continue to preserve the record of her daring deeds, that inspired the valor of her countrymen to follow her to victory, battling for the right.

Every age has had its illustrious women, who typify all that is good and great and worthy of imitation—grand, noble characters, who have continually demonstrated the capability of woman for bearing her share of the responsibilities of her generation.

Foremost among those of her time was that "noble example of womanhood," Lucretia Mott, whose life was beautified by her works of love for humanity and peace ; who yet could perceive "the sense of duty " actuating those who conscientiously responded to the call of their country in her hour of danger and trial, for was it not in consequence of the unfaithfulness of those upon whom the responsibility rested of resisting in the councils of the nation, the encroachments of the slave power toward the domination of all its interests and powers that led to secession and war ? And she could recognize the righteous retribution that entailed the stern duty of the defence of the government in the interest of liberty and peace, on the part of those who had not yet reached her own standpoint of dependence upon the righteous judgments of God in all things.

Recognizing in woman the abilities and the qualities that have shown her to be in possibilities, the co-equal with man in all the interests and experiences of life, yet is she still denied the place she should occupy—equality of representation before the law and in the race of life with man. An equality that shall include "the twain, united as one flesh," neither a complete or finished being when divided in interest or feeling from the unit that computes our common humanity.

Will any one in this audience seriously question the statement which I shall venture to present, as the sum of all the experiences which belong unto the survivors of a war that desolated the nation for more than four years, who—returning from the scenes of strife, left behind us more than four hundred thousand of our comrades who died for their country, and having with us our maimed and crippled fellow-soldiers, who are yet scattered up and down in the land—remain to be the only competent witnesses capable of making a true estimate which living men may venture to make. Surely *we* may be justified if we should realize that no other age or conflict presented in history, can exhibit so vivid and terrible a picture of suffering, of toil and of patient endurance that could preserve the faith and hold fast unto hope through more than four years of weary, devastating war, attended by privations that might well appall the stoutest hearts.

Yet is there a man of us all who—measuring his own share of what he saw, of what he felt, of what he did, of what he knew and what he was, as a part of all this picture of war and its desolation at the front and upon the fields of battle—will say that all this that we endured was comparable unto that unutterable woe of heart and life that was the daily and hourly experience during all those weary years of uncertainty, of fear, of care and of anxious waiting in the silent and desolate home, out from which had gone the son, the husband, the brother, the father, whom the agonized mothers, wives, sisters and daughters mourned for, prayed for and hoped for, with a love stronger than death, during all those sorrowful days of suffering, wherein their hands might not relax from the toil and the duty of keeping the home and providing for the little ones left to their protection and nurture? For them there was no element of exciting activity to relieve or dispel the sense of pain and the heart-gnawing, amid doubts and fears, that could only be made less wearing by the certainty that brought the knowledge of death ; that told of the rest and peace in the distant grave ; of toil and pain and suffering ended.

Surely those who thus endured were the *real heroes* of the war ! All honor to them for the blessing of their tears and their prayers that followed and watched over us, and for their ministrations sent forth into the field, where the tender, loving care of their mitigating hands came, bringing ease to pain and balm to the heart and staunching to the flow of waning life with a devotion that has caused the fame of our corps of nurses to keep pace with the valor of our bravest in the field. The names of Miss Dix and Clara Barton are world renowned, and we have yet with us here to-day our own honored Mother St. John.

The cheer of woman's presence within the tent, beside the dying comrade in his last hours, has softened the bitterness of death through the comfort of the soothing hand that, when all was over, should write the last sad message of love that was to bear the tidings to distant ones, of the love and faith that whispered a cherished name in the last moments of life with an interest that ensures the meeting beyond the gates with the absent, unforgotten ones.

Such was the worth and such the work of woman in that crisis of our history as a Nation, that has made it the pivotal period of our existence as a fully tested and well-established government among the nations of the earth.

Shall *we* not therefore do ourselves the justice of showing a most full and perfect recognition of *woman*, not as a mere cipher, filling out the initial importance of an integer, by one, more or less, o (cipher) at the *left* hand of the statement, but placed in the *right* and at the even level of her worth wherever *she* may indicate her ability to impress a characteristic ?

Shall *we* venture to limit her in the exercise of her gifts and her talents in these days of progress, or in *this* presence, where we have come together to recall the incidents and the interests of our eventful service during the war ?

Is there one of *us* who can remain unconscious of the moisture of an uprising tear that dims the eye when he remembers, amid the scenes of the past which this occasion recalls, the parting sorrows and the tears which could no longer be restrained when the last embrace and the farewell kiss had passed between the loved ones of every kin, never so dear as at the parting ?

Nor shall we ever cease to remember the joyous welcome these devoted ones gave to those of us who returned to receive the blessing of their rejoicing and thanksgiving.

But I pause now before the sad contrast of the sacred sorrow of those, borne down by the weight of their untold grief, whose loved ones returned not to receive their welcome, and whose tears of mourning now, as then, will receive an added impulse from these renewed memories. Unto these our tenderest sympathies go forth, and they will know that, though others may forget them and their sorrows, the comrades of their beloved dead will never grow indifferent to the memory of those who fell in our holy cause.

God bless them, and keep us true to them and to a worthy appreciation of woman not only in sentiment but in verity, as "God's best" and holiest gift to life and love.

THIRD REGULAR TOAST.

"'Brandywine,' 'Paoli,' and 'Valley Forge.' Reminders of heroic deeds and patriotic suffering."

"Old Continentals in their ragged uniforms never faltered."

Assigned to Captain William Wayne, Co. K, who responded as follows :

It is not now, Mr. President, necessary to recount the story of the American Revolution, but only so much of it as bears upon the sentiment just proposed.

The grouping of Brandywine, Paoli and Valley Forge seems appropriate in consideration of their geographical and territorial relations. They all lie within our county limits ; but this grouping also brings before us a very interesting feature in our history, in that in their association they present to us one of the gloomiest periods in our struggle for political independence and for civil, religious and political rights.

You will remember that, after the occupancy of New York by the British troops, there yet remained one grand purpose of General Howe unachieved—the capture of the city of Philadelphia—which, when accomplished, it was hoped, along with the annihilation of their main army, would break down the rebellious opposition to His Majesty in the middle Colonies. To this end the enemy overran New Jersey from the latter part of '76 to the middle of June, '77, battling and skirmishing with alternating success and failure, but without succeeding in forcing Washington into a battle upon their own terms. Failing in this, they betook themselves again to New York.

The many and different feints of the British general from this time forth greatly embarrassed General Washington. It was reported that the Howes, with a considerable force, had sailed— destination, the capes of Delaware. Washington collected his troops and marched for Philadelphia, only to learn that again he had been deceived.

The enemy had headed for the Chesapeake, and disembarked at the head of Elk, and at Chadds Ford, on the Brandywine, Washington presented himself to oppose their further march to Philadelphia. A battle ensued. Defeat of the American troops was the result, and they retired demoralized and despondent.

We now come to Paoli. All that Washington now felt capable of doing was the harassing of the enemy's troops on their march to the city. The prevention of its occupation by them had been virtually given up as hopeless.

In the latter part of September a large detachment of the enemy lay along the south valley range of hills in the neighborhood of the present Howelville and New Centreville, and about three miles from Paoli. A force was detailed by Washington to take position near and hang upon their rear, with the view of cutting off their baggage and otherwise impeding their march. Every pre-

(4)

caution was taken by the American officer in command for the security of his camp, and its location was believed to be unknown to the enemy. On the night of the 20th of September, piloted by an enemy to the patriot cause, General Grey reached the camp, and committed what has ever been recognized as one of the most barbarous butcherings of modern times.

This affair is called in many of our histories the "Surprise at Paoli," but investigation of the subject at the time showed that, so far from being a surprise, the American troops were on the alert and in position when the white savages came on the ground, and that this most inhuman and unjustifiable massacre was due to disobedience, neglect or misapprehension of orders on the part of a subordinate officer.

After much marching and countermarching, General Howe took possession of Philadelphia September 26th.

In October following one serious attempt was made to redeem the city, and at Germantown fortune again failed to smile on the American arms. An accident alone saved His Majesty's army from a signal defeat.

On December 17th the American army took up its position at Valley Forge and went into camp. Into the details of life there (if life it can be called) I will not enter ; they are familiar to you all. It was a campaign not against flesh and blood, against cannon and cutlass, but more terrible than these—against cold, hunger, naked-ness and disease.

The language of exaggeration fails to describe the terrible realities of life in the camp of the Patriot Army in '77 and '78.

The poet, the painter, the historian have come short in depicting the sufferings and the trials of the

"Old Continentals in their ragged regimentals"

during the long and dark and dreary winter at Valley Forge.

FOURTH REGULAR TOAST.

"The Union of the States, the glory of the past and the hope of our future."

"Our country's welfare our first concern."

To Colonel John Wainwright.

Mr. Chairman : It seems like presumption for me to attempt a response to such a toast on an occasion like this. "Our country's welfare our first concern " is well attested by the armless, legless and shattered remnants of brave and gallant veterans who are about us here to-day. Our first concern for our country's welfare was well attested when in our youth, three and twenty years ago, we first trod the sod of this enclosure to the tap of drum and the "left! left! left!" of our squad commanders in our preparations for what proved a long four years of bitter struggle and strife, of hardship, privations, disease and death.

Our first concern for our country's welfare was well attested, Mr. Chairman, when, on a beautiful sunlight morning in November nearly a quarter of a century ago, a train of cars with these veterans drew out from yonder station for the seat of war, leaving behind us weeping and broken-hearted mothers, wives, sisters and daughters, who gave the brightest gems of their families a sacrifice for their country's welfare.

Our first concern for our country's welfare was magnificently attested before Secessionville; before Wagner, Gregg and Sumter, Green Plains, Cold Harbor, Petersburg, Fort Fisher and a score of other conflicts with treason and rebellion. It was well attested, sir, by faithful services in the Army of the South, the Army of the James, the Army of the Potomac, and with Sherman in the Army of the Ohio.

The three hundred and five dead of the gallant old Regiment, well attests our first concern for our country's welfare, scattered in every State from Massachusetts to Florida. One at least sleeps in the billowy Atlantic. Who of these survivors does not remember the solemn occasion of his funeral on shipboard? Some sleep in ever-green graves of Florida; some in Georgia chaperell; some in Carolina's sands, on Virginia's bloody battlefields, in Southern prison grounds and in Northern hospital cemeteries; some came home to die, nursed by loving hearts and tender hands; some sleep on yonder hillside, almost within the sound of my voice, whose graves you so fondly decorate on the annual return of each Memorial Day.

"Our first concern for our country's welfare" is well attested, sir, by the four hundred and fifty-eight wounded and crippled of the Ninety-seventh Pennsylvania Volunteers, who are scattered all over this land as living but shattered monuments of their fidelity to their country and first concern for its welfare.

Mr. Chairman, "our first concern for our country's welfare" is well attested by these survivors, who, after having borne the heat of battle and breasted scores of storms of leaden hail, and after a separation of twenty years, have come here to-day to the very spot where we had our first instruction for our country's defence in the duties of the soldier, to renew and reassert our "concern for our country's welfare;" to greet our comrades of yore with hearty hand-shake and fond embrace, and to bid them God-speed for the future.

As I look into these dear old faces, after twenty years of separation, they grow more and more familiar, and the full, round, boyish faces of twenty years ago come back to me, and the interval seems but yesterday. God grant, Mr. Chairman and dear old comrades, that this Reunion of the survivors of the gallant old Ninety-seventh Pennsylvania Regiment may be annually repeated until the grave of the last survivor shall be decked with the sweetest flowers of spring.

FIFTH REGULAR TOAST.

"The touch of the elbow; the scenes and memories of twenty years ago."

"Should auld acquaintance be forgot
And never brought to mind?"

This toast was assigned to Dr. Theo. Worrall of Co. B, who responded most eloquently as follows:

Mr. President and Comrades: My position here is a lonely one, being the only private soldier who has been called upon to-day; but I feel encouraged when I look into the faces of my comrades, and feel that my remarks, coming from the heart and not the head, will be received with the kindliest feeling. [Applause.]

Only a short time since I was notified that the toast and sentiment just announced was assigned to me, and that I would be expected to respond. My first impulse was to refuse: being surrounded by the weighty cares of a busy professional life. I felt it impossible to give the subject proper thought and attention. But when I sat down to write a reply, how vividly the scenes and memories of twenty years ago passed before me! In file, in section, in platoon, in columns of companies they passed in panoramic review, and I felt that I must come here, and in my feeble way help to erect a temple in our hearts to the stirring scenes of auld lang syne. [Applause.] And why should we not do this? Are not those memories burned in living letters on our mind? And are they not worthy of commemoration? For twenty-three centuries the human family has paid tribute to great men and great deeds. A beautiful marble edifice, called the Hall of Heroes, in which repose the effigies of the great men of all Germany, stands on the

Danube, that historic river whose shores have listened to the hymns of the Crusaders, resounded with the tread of Roman Legions, and trembled under the thunder of Napoleon's artillery. William Tell's memory is perpetuated by a chapel on the shores of the placid Lake Lucerne. A statue of Andrew Hofer wins thither the weary feet of the peasant of the Tyrol to the dark aisles of the Cathedral at Innspruck. In our Nation's Capital stands a magnificent monument, whose capstone pierces the ethereal blue of the heavens, erected to the memory of the man after whom the city is named. [Applause.]

Then, I ask, why should not we erect in our hearts a rich, rare monument to the memories of days passed forever? I ask you to give me the touch of the elbow as of yore. Let the subtle cords of memory carry you back over the years since the nation's fate hung in the balance, and bring to mind scenes and memories of twenty years ago. Time has written great chapters in the history of nations since then. The elastic step is gone with which you sprang into line when the electric current flashed through the North the question pure and simple, Shall this country be preserved? [Applause] The great artist Time has penciled silver threads in your locks since the day you fought for national unity. Yet how vivid the memories! It seems but yesterday that the dear old Ninety-seventh Regiment stood on this ground an undisciplined and awkward body of men, but with hearts aglow with patriotic enthusiasm. But yesterday that Pennsylvania's great-hearted War Governor [Applause]—than whom a better never lived—presented us with the flag—that flag the emblem of our nationality, and for which we suffered so many dangers and hardships. Our first dress parade, and the day Colonel Duer kept us one hour at a shoulder arms, while the Adjutant read orders. [Laughter and applause.] Ah, the poor Adjutant! Sacred be his memory! [Emotional applause.] Methinks I hear the awkward challenge of the equally awkward sentinel, and the many schemes we resorted to when we wanted to break the guard and get into West Chester. And (turning to Colonel Guss), Colonel, what brilliant flank movements we would make down an alley when we would spy you coming down the street. [Great applause.] These are all memories of twenty years ago. Time has not dimmed the recollection of our departure to the seat of war. The leave-takings, the fond embraces, the tears, the benedictions, how vividly these scenes arise! In fancy I yet see the mother—that *dear old loyal* mother. With a heart bursting as she contemplated the uncertainties of the future; with hands raised toward heaven; with cheeks wet with tears of maternal love, she asked God to protect her boy. This is no fancy sketch. If you think so, go with me to the fireside where sits that mother, whose form is bent with age, whose locks are silvered with the snows of many winters, and ask her if there was not a stern reality in the parting of twenty odd years ago.

Then, again, I ask you to follow me along the line of march from West Philadelphia to the Cooper Shop Refreshment Saloon. Ah, boys, I think you can remember those knapsacks we carried, loaded so full of the *unnecessaries* of a soldier's life that they would break down any mule General Grant had in Virginia. [Applause.] Then that passage through the flagless, treason-tainted streets of Baltimore ; the pitching of tents for the first time, under the shadows of the Nation's Capital ; the exchange of arms at the arsenal ; then back to Baltimore, and, oh, heavens ! that voyage from there to the sun-bathed shores of South Carolina. Will you ever forget it ? Why, the very thought of it makes a fellow feel as if he had taken a dose of tartar emetic. [Great applause.] How we threw up everything except the Government shoes we had on our feet. [Applause and laughter.] How we remember the campaigns in the heart of the South—Port Royal, Fernandina, Jacksonville. How clearly we see all this ! The enemy for the first time ! How every nerve thrilled as with electric fire when you looked down the gleaming rifle barrels into their faces, and how confidently you felt the touch of the elbow of comrades tried and true on right and left. Then the first dead comrade ! Has this scene been forgotten ? I see him yet. The gallant Henry Dunn, Co. B, died doing his duty at Grimball's Plantation, June 10th, 1862. I think he was the first man killed in the Regiment. Then comes Morris Island, the siege of Sumter—that spot made memorable, yes, and damnable, by Americans who, forgetting the traditions of the past, that love of country born in the womb of a *British despot's tyranny, baptized in the blood of their patriotic sires in 1776*, fired with malicious disloyalty on the American flag. [Applause.] It was there where, asleep or awake, we were continually under a storm of bursting iron. No foot of that island withdrawn from the enemy's sight—no foot but what could be played upon with rebel shot and shell as a piano's keys under Thalberg's stormy fingers.

Comrades, would you want to forget those scenes and memories of twenty years ago ? No ! Let us hold them sacred. Methinks, did I want to, I would ask the gods to let me die. [Applause.] Follow me to Virginia, where battles, sieges and bivouacs followed in one ceaseless round. Richmond, Petersburg, Fort Fisher, how clearly we see it all! This day dead comrades ; that day bearing off a bloody field the form of a beloved Major, stricken with many wounds. [Applause.] These memories are not the idle *phantasmagoria* of an over-excited brain, but living memories of stirring scenes of twenty years ago, and reason must have forsaken its throne in the man who has forgotten them. [Applause.] Like the noonday sun breaking through the storm-cloud, bathing the earth in a bright sheen of glory, these memories come o'er me, and, bright though they be, my heart is saddened by others. On the slopes of the sunny Southland ; by the rippling waves of the winding James ; on North Carolina's billow-beaten coast, rest those whose triumphs, defeats and trials have ended. Then let us pause in the midst of the festive scenes of to-day, and while the autumnal winds, soughing through the dying verdure of the forest, sings a sad requiem over their graves, consecrate one memory, one thought, to our dead comrades—the absent ones with whom we touched elbows twenty years ago ! [Applause.] Their death carried grief and sorrow into many households. Hearts, stricken and desolate, bowed at the fireside, and 'tis useless to try to swing the burden clear of any heart by throwing into the scale on the other hand the vast amount of captured cannon, or the number of prisoners taken. It will not lighten the load one ounce. [Applause.] But this thought may: their death helped to establish on a firm basis and forever, that government without a model ; that government without a prototype, and to place that flag (here a piece of the old regimental flag, shot away at the battle of Green Plains, Va., was shown), the fairest blossom in all the flowery world, to blooming in its native soil once more. [Great applause.]

Now, comrades, I implore you to keep alive these memories and scenes of twenty years ago. Do not forget that you once composed a part of that army which gained an individuality attained by none other of which history tells. [Applause.] Hurled time after time by incompetent general officers against impregnable works, beaten back in a shapeless mass, yet ever ready to place its bleeding bosom between danger and its country, and beat back the billows of rebellion, in spray tinged with its life blood, to the lair from which they came. [Applause.] Napoleon once said, in a burst of haughty eloquence, " In all the great armies of Europe the commander was everything." " It was not," said he, " the Roman army that conquered Gaul, but Cæsar ; it was not the Carthagenian army

L. of C.

that made Rome tremble at her gates, but Hannibal ; it was not the
Macedonian army that marched to the Indies, but Alexander ; it
was not the Prussian army that beat back from her borders three of
the most powerful armies of Europe, but Frederick " This proud
apotheosis has no application to the Army of the Union. In it no
central figure arose to become the cynosure of all eyes. 'Tis true
the names of Grant, Sherman, Meade, Sheridan and Pennsylvania's
gallant sons, Hancock and Reynolds, stand prominently [great
applause] the peer of any of the great military chieftains of Europe,
yet they are but the perspective of the picture, the bold outlines of
which is that gallant army that dared to do and die for God's own
country. [Applause.]

Now, let me say in conclusion, let us keep up this touch of the
elbow ; let us once in every twelve months meet here and recall the
scenes and memories of twenty years ago ; and may the anniversary
of this day be a bright flower, pure as the calla, to place in our
garland of years. [Applause.]

SIXTH REGULAR TOAST.

" The men of the 97th Pennsylvania Volunteers, who died that
the Republic might live. The mystic chords of memory that stretch
from every battle-field."

> " O'er fame's eternal camping ground
> Their silent tents are spread,
> And Glory guards, with solemn round,
> The bivouac of the dead."

Assigned to Captain Geo. A. Lemaistre, who responded as
follows :

Mr. President and Comrades: At this time I cannot prevent
memory taking me back twenty-three years, when with hearts full
of patriotic fire, we first greeted each other on this ground. But I
look in vain for the faces of many noble ones who were then with us.
The handshakings of to-day but recall more vividly to each of us
the absent ones.

The joy of our meeting is mingled with melancholy thoughts
of those who gave their lives that this country might live. Their
patriotism, fidelity and courage can never fail to be cherished. The
brave and faithful Durnell, the modest and patriotic Watkins, the
unflinching courage of our beloved Carruthers and the daring and
impetuous Hawkins will ever be green in our memory.

Our death roll is long and illustrious. In almost every southern state our heroic comrades have fallen. Their names will be cherished not only by us, but by their posterity until the end of time.

All honor to the glorious dead whose devotion to their country has taught a lesson too solemn to be forgotten. Their names with their deeds will ever be held in reverence by a grateful people.

———

The responses to the toasts were all very eloquently delivered and each of those responding was liberally applauded. Comrade Worrall's response to " The touch of the elbow," although entirely impromptu, was decidedly appropriate and in it he recalled many pleasant reminiscences of the days when the comrades' elbows touched while in line for the preservation of The Union.

After the conclusion of the regular toasts many of the comrades were gathered about the stand occupied by the music and sang, accompanied by the orchestra, many of the stirring and patriotic songs of the war, which seemed to intensify the feeling of comradeship and unforgetfulness of the old times when they sang together around the camp-fire to cheer the loneliness of those days of toil and service. And then came the closing scene at the banquetting hall, and really the last feature on the programme—a song by comrade Ray of Philadelphia. This over, the meeting terminated in many cheers for comrades and officers that made the hall resound with echoes, such as never were heard in " Old Camp Wayne " since the boys left it in 1861.

The carrying out of the programme was so successful that it exceeded the expectations of the most sanguine, and much credit is due the following executive committee having the matter in charge :

L. R. Thomas, Samuel Hawley, John A. Groff, David Jones, D. W. C. Lewis, S. A. March, Oliver Channell, I. A. Cleaver, Captain Underwood and others.

At 4 P. M. the drum and fife were again heard sounding the recall. Colonel Price again called upon the comrades in the old-time way—" Fall in, boys," when the march was resumed up Church to Market, to High, to Gay. When at the old landmark the line was halted, and faced to the front, Colonel Price spoke these parting words : "Comrades, we are about to separate, but only for another year, when we will all meet again, I hope, our ranks undiminished I trust, and our locks not much the whiter in the interval. I feel that I shall voice the sentiment of every one of us here when I say we have had a most grand and enjoyable time, and that our Re-union has been a most magnificent and gratifying success. Good-bye, comrades, God bless you all ; but before we disperse there is one name that we have heard spoken to-day, more than once, in terms of honor and love, whose absence we have felt and regretted ; one now far away at Hot Springs, Ark., where he has gone to seek healing for his wounds—Brevet-Major General G. Pennypacker, U. S. Army. I ask you to give three cheers for him." These were given with a will. Three cheers were then given to our old Fife-major, C. Fah-nestock, our host of the Green Tree Hotel. Three cheers were given for Mother St. John ; three cheers for all the survivors and three for Col. Price. Then once more the boys disbanded and returned to their homes.

The Roster.

Colonel Henry R. Guss, West Chester.
Lieutenant-Colonel A. P. Duer, Atglen.
Colonel John Wainwright, Wilmington, Del.
Brevet-Colonel Isaiah Price, Philadelphia.
Adjutant Elwood P. Baldwin, West Chester.
Quartermaster David Jones, West Chester.
Quartermaster John H. Brower, Vincent.
Chaplain D. W. Moore, Kennett Square.
Sergeant-Major Samuel W. Hawley, Media.
Fife-Major Casper C. Fahnestock, West Chester.

BAND.

Bernard Roecker, West Chester.
Thomas H. Windle, Coatesville.
Wm. H. H. Taylor, Chester, Del. Co.
William Dalling, West Chester.
John L. Hosmer, Newtown Square.

COMPANY A.

Captain Francis M. Guss, West Chester.
First Lieutenant William Peace, Coatesville.
First Lieutenant Abel Griffith, West Chester.
First Lieutenant Harry T. Gray, Philadelphia.
Sergeant Jeptha Clark, Coatesville.
Corporal Reese Elmer Welch, Cedar Knoll.
Corporal Madison Lovett, Oxford.
Musician Edward R. Eisenbeis, Philadelphia.
Teamster Isaac P. Chandler, Ercildoun.
Private Alexander M. Chandler, Chester Valley.
    "   James Y. Clark, Coatesville.
    "   Isaac M. Pawling,   "
    "   Robert H. Humpton, Coatesville.
    "   Joseph P. Robinson, Curwensville.
    "   Lafayette Thompson, London Grove.
    "   George W. Hawkins, Wilmington, Del.
    "   Joseph G. Brower,   "   "
    "   George W. Cass, Sugartown.
    "   John A. Groff, West Chester.
    "   William H. H. Starts, West Chester.
    "   John W. Dowlin, Coatesville.
    "   William Mercer, Talcose.
    "   Dr. Joseph E. Valentine, Philadelphia.

Private Ephraim L. Ross, Philadelphia.
" George P. Matthews, "
" Ezra G. Goodwin, Frazer.
" David M. Taylor, Oxford.
" Jeremiah King, "
" Isaac W. Gray, Glen Olden, Del. Co.
" Joseph Winkler, Manayunk.
" Richard E. Pharaoh, Phœnixville.

COMPANY B.

Captain Dallas Crow, Philadelphia.
Second Lieutenant John B. Griffith, Modena.
1st. Sergeant Webster A. Nichols, Unionsville.
Sergeant Nelson P. Boyer, Coatesville.
" Harvey Highet, Fairmount, Lancaster Co.
" James M. Jackson Cowan, Oxford.
" Gerhart Reeder, West Chester.
Corporal Robert Bruce Wallace, Philadelphia.
Private Amor N. Chalfant, Christiana, Lancaster Co.
" Samuel J. Day, Coatesville.
" George Doubts, "
" Joseph Emerson, Cochranville.
" Edmund Esrey, Philadelphia.
" Wesley Vance, "
" Jacob D. Lemley, "
" Albert Harkins, Compassville.
" Dr. Theodore A. Worrall, North East, Md.
" George G. Supplee, Honeybrook.

COMPANY C.

Captain Leonard R. Thomas, West Chester.
First Lieut. Emmor G. Griffith, "
" " George W. Abel, Concordville.
" " Charles Warren, Valley Forge.
Sergeant Isaac A. Cleaver, Berwyn.
" B. Lundy Kent, (Capt. 13th Heavy Art'y, U. S.
C. T.,) Wilmington, Del.
" Stephen H. Eachus, West Chester.
" Cyrus M. Davis, Wagontown.
Corporal Davis O. Taylor, West Chester.
" Levis T. Beidler, Cambria Station.
" C. Burleigh Hambleton, Elk View.
" Maris Pierce, Sioux City, Iowa.
" John R. Miller, Downingtown.
" Jesse D. Farra, West Chester.
Private Oliver B. Channel, "
" Samuel Woodward, "
" Emmor B. Hickman, "
" Samuel A. March, "

Private J. Jones Still, Malvern.
" James J. Dewees, New Centreville.
" Eugene Vickers, Philadelphia.
" Edward Mendenhall, "
" Ambrose Quay, Birchrunville.
" Elwood Griffith, Rock Island, Ill.
" William H. Speakman, W. Whiteland.
" Robert A. Wilson, Cochranville.
" William Whistler, Warren Tavern.
" William D. Thomas, Downingtown.

COMPANY D.

Captain Isaac B. Taylor, Columbia.
Second Lieutenant John W. Brooks, Coatesville.
Sergeant Samuel McBride, Frankford, Philadelphia.
" John E. Davis, Philadelphia.
Corporal Robert Fairlamb, Elwyn, Del. Co.
" John Goodwin, Wilmington, Del.
" John Jordan, Wilmington, Del.
" John W. Carter, Elam, Del. Co.
Teamster Francis W. Starkey, Aston Mills, Del. Co.
Private W. W. Bullock, Wilmington, Del.
" Francis M. Frame, Parkesburg.
" John Dowlin, Thurlow, Del. Co.
" James Hamilton, Nether Providence.
" John E. Huey, Parkerville.
" Edward Maxwell, Greenville, Del. Co.
" Francis H. Pyle, Glen Mills, Del. Co.
" Walter Pyle, Cheyney, Del. Co.
" George W. Eavenson, Thornton, Del. Co.
" Abram Fawkes, Malvern.
" John Pass, Chaddsford.
" Samuel J. Cloud, West Chester.
" William W. McIntosh, Downingtown.
" James Beaumont, Glen Riddle, Del. Co.
" William Beaumont, Chester, Delaware Co.
" Richard S. Howarth, Media, "

COMPANY E.

Second Lieut John Sullivan, West Chester.
Sergeant George L. Smith, "
" James A. Riley, Coatesville.
Corporal George Jenkins, West Chester.
Musician Charles Riley, "
Private Robert Sherman, Glen Hall.
" Francis Hilderbrant, Danville, Pa.
" Callum [Colom] Duffy, Wilmington, Del.
" Thomas Dallas, Parkesburg.

COMPANY F.

Brevet-Lieut. Colonel D. W. C. Lewis, West Chester.
Captain Lewis P. Malin, St. Davids, Pa.
First Lieut. Isaac J. Nichols, Port Kennedy, Pa.
Second Lieut. Thomas Cosgriff, West Chester.
    "   " John E. Huntsman, Sugartown.
First Sergeant Thomas E. Brown, Wilmington, Del.
Sergeant Samuel Wynn, Nantmeal Village.
    " Herman P. Brower, West Whiteland.
Corporal Edward Townsend, Philadelphia.
    " Joseph R. Richardson, Saddsburyville.
    " Jesse M. Boyles, West Chester.
    " Henry C. Reagan,   "
Private Evan Pharaoh,   "
    " Hugh Hale,   "
    " William T. Meeteer, Modena.
    " John W. Keeley, Spring City.
    " William E. Stiteler, Columbia.
    " Abraham Thomas, Henry Clay, Del.
    " Edward Shewey, Lickdale, Pa.

COMPANY G.

Captain Caleb Hoopes, Media.
    " Washington W. James, Darby, Del. Co.
First Lieut. Gasway O. Yarnall, Chester, Del. Co.
Second Lieut. William H. Eves,   "   "
First Sergeant Franklin P. Clapp, Media.
Sergeant Charles E. Ottey,   "
    " Thomas J. Wade, Oxford.
    " Thomas S. Dicker, Abrams, Montgomery Co.
Corporal Ezekiel T. Richie, Philadelphia.
    " Hillary Fox, West Chester.
    " Eli Dunlap, Landenberg, Del.
    " John S. Culbert, Chester, Del.
Private Crosley B. Wilson, Media.
    " William Popjoy,   "
    " Alexander Miller, Crum Lynn, Delaware Co.
    " George White, Marple, Delaware Co.
    " Philip Rothwein, Roxborough, Philadelphia.

COMPANY H.

Captain George A. LeMaistre, Wilmington, Del.
    " Theodore M. Smedley,   "   "
Sergeant Robert J. Baldwin, Pottstown, Montgomery Co.
    " Robert Walker, Downingtown.
Corporal Thomas W. Durnall, Collamer.
    " William F. Smith, Conshohocken.
Teamster Marshall B. England, West Chester.
    " Levi F. Snyder, Glen Moore.

Private Alfred C. Allison, Downingtown.
"   Isaac B. Davis, Hopewell Cotton Works.
"   John A. D. McKeever, Wilmington, Del.
"   Ezra H. Sullivan,   "   "
"   William M. Steele, Philadelphia.
"   Payne A. Goold, West Chester.

COMPANY I.

Captain George W. Duffee, Moores Station, Delaware Co.
Second Lieut. George M. Middleton, Philadelphia.
Sergeant William R. Wood, Dupont, Del.
"   Jacob Cline, Chester, Del. Co.
Corporal Charles Stewart, Moores Station, Del. Co.
Private Thomas Edwards, Oakdale, Delaware Co.
"   Henry P. Lindsay, Chester Valley.
"   James Groff, Clifton Heights, Delaware Co.
"   James Maloney, Philadelphia.
"   David T. Nuttle, Chester, Delaware Co.
"   Richard Walraven, Ridley, Delaware Co.
"   Isaac D. Haines, Philadelphia.

COMPANY K.

Captain William Wayne, Paoli.
"   William S. Underwood, West Chester.
First Lieut. William M. Sullivan, Warren Tavern.
Second Lieut. Marriott Brosius, Lancaster, Pa.
Sergeant R. Powell, Fithian, West Chester, Pa.
Corporal Barnett R. Rapp,   "   "
"   Isaac Miller, Collamer, Lancaster Co.
"   William E. Davis, Spread Eagle.
Musician John H. Kauffman, Berwyn.
Private John S. Famous, Chester Valley.
"   Isaac Harrison, St. Davids, Pa.
"   Henry B. Thomas, Norristown, Pa.
"   Sebastian Keeley, Birchrunville.
"   Daniel Urmy, West Chester.

[The above list contains the names of all who registered at the office of the Secretary, and such others as could be ascertained. If any who were in attendance are omitted it is owing to their not having attended to the notice to register their names, as it would be otherwise impossible to know who were present.]

WEST CHESTER, Nov., 6TH, 1884.

A meeting of the executive committee of the Society of the Ninety-seventh Pennsylvania Volunteers, was held at the office of John A. Groff, at 2 o'clock, P. M., this date, the chairman, S. W. Hawley, presiding. Present: Wm. S. Underwood, Herman P. Brower, Robert Fairlamb, L. R. Thomas and Samuel A. March of the committee; Colonel H. R. Guss, D. W. C. Lewis, I. A. Cleaver and others also present.

The minutes of the previous meeting were read and approved. The following bills of expenses incurred by the committee, were presented for payment:

	Dr.	Cr.
Rent of Fair Grounds	$ 10.00	
Harry Mills for services at Fair Grounds .	5.00	
D. W. C. Lewis, work preparing tables, stands, etc. at Grounds	21.06	
J. B. Smith, furnishing chairs .	30.00	
W. A. Rollins, decorations in Hall . . .	26.50	
Edward Strong, carriage hire for Orator and Mrs. St. John	6.00	
T. L. Hawkins, Caterer, as per contract	330.00	
T. T. Smith, for cigars . .	15.00	
Charles Jolly, for beer . .	10.00	
H. C. Wood, for music	27.00	
C. C. Fahnestock, entertaining Mrs. St. John and daughter	3.50	
By cash in Treasury from former collections		184.50
" received from subscriptions at meeting		256.00
" contributed by Colonel H. R. Guss		7.26
" " " Lieutenant W. H. Eves		7.26
" " " Sergeant Robert Fairlamb		7.26
" " " " I. A. Cleaver		7.26
" " " Sergeant-major S.W. Hawley		7.26
" " " Captain Wm. Wayne		7.26
	$484.06	$484.06

On motion the above bills, which constitute the entire amount of the cost of the Reunion, were ordered to be paid. The six comrades above named contributing equally to make up a deficiency in the amount collected of $43.56, so as to close the account and settle all bills.

There being a number of subscriptions yet outstanding, the Secretary was directed to collect the same and pay to the Treasurer of the Society. The committee then adjourned its session, to meet at such time and place as the chairman shall direct.

L. R. THOMAS, *Secretary.*

www.ingramcontent.com/pod-product-compliance
Lightning Source LLC
Chambersburg PA
CBHW021629270326
41931CB00008B/945